Steam in Austria
1955–1975

Previous page: Zillertalbahn No 4, built by Krauss, Linz in 1905, is seen shunting at Jenbach in the 1950s. *Author's Collection*

Superheated two-cylinder 2-6-2 compound No 135.335 (StEG 3852/1912), originally kkStB No 429.198, awaits its next turn of duty at Selzthal shed on 10 September 1958. The remaining members of ÖBB Class 135 were withdrawn between 1957 and 1962, with No 135.335 succumbing in February 1960. *John McCann/Online Transport Archive*

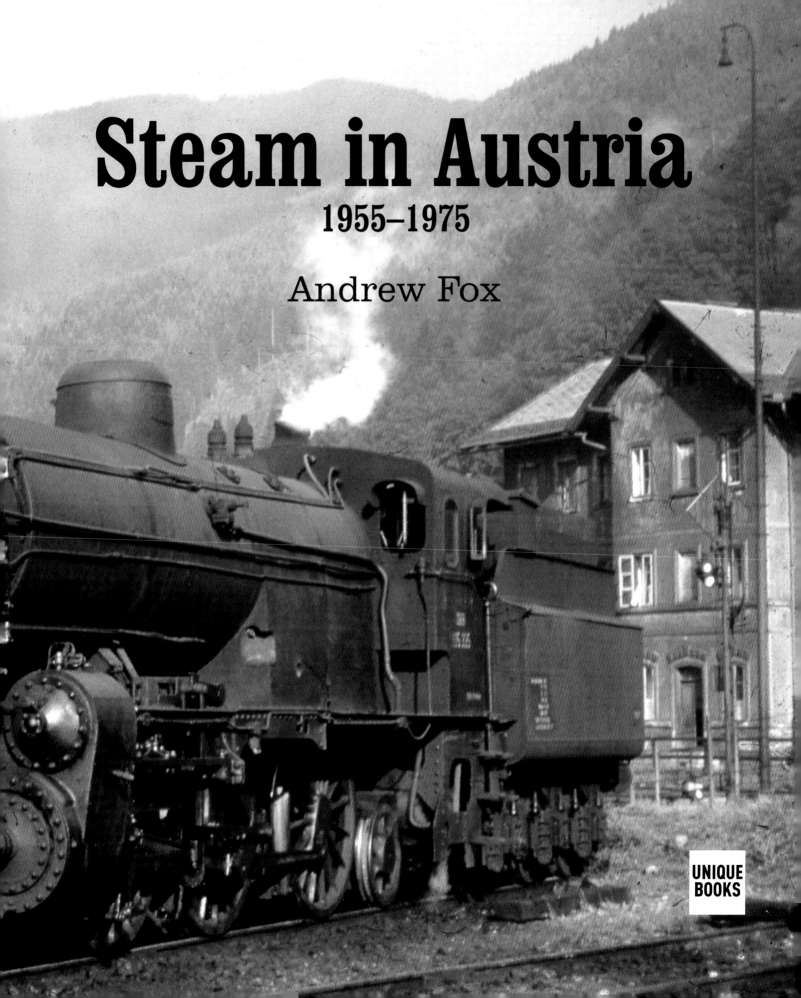

Steam in Austria

1955–1975

Andrew Fox

UNIQUE
BOOKS

Dedication
To Elisabeth Hackl and her late husband Hans, whose friendship and generosity to me contributed greatly to my love of Austria and its fascinating railways. Without them this book would not have been written.

Front Cover: Class 97 No 97.204 climbs above Vordernberg on the Erzbergbahn with a train of empty ore wagons. (see page 62). *Author's Collection*

Back Cover: Standing outside the locomotive shed at Wien Ost (Vienna East), smartly turned out No 52.4553 (DWM 869/1944) is one of 136 ÖBB Class 52/152 locomotives which were fitted with a Giesl ejector in 1956/57. More than 100 bogie tenders were rebuilt by the ÖBB with a guard's cabin, as seen here, and used with members of 2-10-0 Classes 42, 52 and 152. *Author's Collection*

A note on the photographs
Many of the illustrations in this book have been drawn from the collection of the Online Transport Archive, a UK-registered charity that was set up to accommodate collections put together by transport enthusiasts who wished to see their precious images secured for the long-term. Further information about the archive can be found at: www.onlinetransportarchive.org or email secretary@onlinetransportarchive.org

Steam in Austria 1955–1975

Andrew Fox

First published in the United Kingdom by Unique Books 2021

© Text: Author 2021
© Photographs: As credited

ISBN: 978 1 913555 00 9

A CIP record for this book is available from the British Library

Unique Books is an imprint of Unique Publishing Services Ltd, 3 Merton Court, The Strand, Brighton Marina Village, Brighton BN2 5XY.

www.uniquebooks.pub

Printed in Poland

Contents

Foreword

This book covers the period between 1955 and 1975 – a time of great change on Austria's railways, which witnessed the advance of electrification and diesel traction, the progressive disappearance of the steam locomotive, which by the 1970s had retreated to its final strongholds, and the closure of the first narrow gauge lines.

Deliberately, no attempt is made to bring up to date the history of the various lines and locomotives that are illustrated, and the text does not cover the many changes (modernisation, closures, preservation, etc), which have occurred over subsequent years. These events are not the subject of the following pages; instead, we travel back in time to the period 1955–1975, to a world that has now long disappeared. If the reader is interested in the years following 1975, or in diesel and electric traction in Austria, these subjects are well covered in other books, some of which can be found in the Bibliography on page 160.

I am greatly indebted to the photographers whose work appears on the pages of this book. Particular mention is due to John McCann and Charles Firminger, whose photographs, which are part of the Online Transport Archive collection, play an especially important role on the following pages. Photographers are credited, wherever their identities are known, but in some instances they could unfortunately not be identified.

Andrew Fox
July 2021

Former times at Bruck an der Mur station. *Author's Collection*

Introduction

Land der Berge, Land am Strome ('Land of mountains, land beside the river') are the first words of the Austrian national anthem, but appropriate as this may be, during the 1950s-70s, Austria became increasingly known to railway enthusiasts as, amongst other things, the land of the 760mm narrow gauge, the Semmeringbahn over the Alps, the Erzbergbahn, the Graz-Köflacher Bahn and the Giesl ejector.

In those years Austria had a great deal that was of interest to the railway enthusiast. In addition to wonderful and varied scenery, as well as the hospitality of its people, it offered remarkably engineered lines and a wide variety of sometimes veteran motive power. At the same time it was the home of one of the last major developments in steam locomotive technology, and the location of some of the last steam operations in Western Europe, on both standard and narrow gauges.

Austria and its Railways in the Post-war Era

It is perhaps appropriate that the period covered by this book starts in 1955, the year when the present Austrian republic came into being. Considerable damage had been inflicted on Austria's infrastructure by intensive air raids in the latter part of the war and, as was the case in large parts of Europe, in the 1950s the railways of Austria were still recovering from the damage incurred during hostilities. By the end of the war, large parts of the motive power, rolling stock and infrastructure were severely run-down, and had often been the subject of considerable damage and destruction. As an example of this, in September 1945 fewer than 25% of the 2,744 standard gauge steam locomotives in Austria were in service. The great majority were either under overhaul, waiting for works attention, or so run-down or damaged, that they were beyond practical repair. At many stations, goods yards, depots and workshops, things were just as bleak. The main works at Linz and Floridsdorf were particularly badly affected by the effects of the war.

This situation was addressed vigorously over the years that followed, and significant progress was made with electrifying major lines (notably the Westbahn to Vienna in 1952, and the Semmeringbahn in 1959), and with the introduction of new diesel and electric classes.

In 1955 the ÖBB standard gauge steam fleet consisted of 1,435 locomotives belonging to 78 classes, although by no means all of these were serviceable. Amongst them there were classes dating back to the late 19th and early 20th centuries, with an eclectic mixture of designs including older kaiserlich-königliche Staatsbahnen (kkStB) and Südbahn classes and large numbers of BBÖ designs dating from the 1920s and 1930s. In contrast, both the standard and narrow gauge steam fleets had been revitalized through inheriting former Deutsche Reichsbahn (DR) and Heeresfeldbahn (military) locomotives at the end of the war. On the standard gauge there were powerful and versatile 2-10-0s of Classes 42, 50 and 52, of which members of Class 52 would survive to the end of main line steam. In addition, members of the Reichsbahn standard 2-8-2T Class 86 put in many years of valuable service, together with various older German designs.

On the narrow gauge there were still 67 steam locomotives of 19 classes on the books of the national railway system, if by no means all in service, including the Schneeberg and Schafberg metre gauge rack locomotives. As on the standard gauge, the native designs had been supplemented by various former military locomotives which found themselves on Austrian territory at the end of the war.

10 years later, by 1965, the standard gauge steam fleet had fallen by almost 47% to 712 locomotives, belonging to just 31 classes. As early as August 1965 the last ÖBB express steam locomotive was taken out of service, in the shape of Knittelfeld shed's Class 33 4-8-0 No 33.102.

During the period covered by this volume the ÖBB had three steam locomotive works: Linz (until 1956), Floridsdorf (until 1968), and finally Knittelfeld, which was responsible for the remaining standard and narrow gauge classes until the end of steam.

Decline of the Narrow Gauge

Although closures were limited, a number of narrow gauge lines did succumb, starting in 1957 with perhaps the most sadly missed of them all – the Salzkammergut-Lokalbahn. Declining traffic and a lack of investment led to gradual retrenchment and to the closure of several ÖBB narrow gauge lines, with the loss of both the Vellachtalbahn and Gurktalbahn by the early 1970s. The Steiermärkische Landesbahnen's various lines continued in operation, but passenger services started to disappear, and several lines suffered cut-backs.

A late Rejuvenation for the Steam Locomotive

In the 1950s Austria produced one of the most significant of the later developments to the steam locomotive in the form of the Giesl ejector, designed by Dr Adolph Giesl-Gieslingen. This distinctive modification consisted of a narrow, flat chimney with a large number of separate, small blastpipes, which generated greatly improved draft compared to a conventional blastpipe. Whilst its aesthetic properties were debatable, its practical benefits were beyond dispute. Often combined with a superheat booster mechanism, it delivered significantly enhanced performance, together with reduced fuel consumption and a reduction in spark throwing.

The first ÖBB locomotive to be fitted with a Giesl ejector, in October 1951, was No 33.107 (at the time numbered T33.107). Over an eight-year period the ÖBB fitted Giesl ejectors to a total of 452 locomotives, including a number of narrow gauge locomotives of Classes 499 and 699.1, and the Class 999 and 999.1 rack locomotives. Despite the impending decline of steam power, the Giesl ejector achieved significant sales in a number of other countries.

The Last Years of Steam

By 1970 the ÖBB standard gauge steam fleet had been reduced by a further 39% compared with 1965, and now numbered just 431 locomotives, belonging to 14 classes. By 1975, only Classes 52, 77 and

93 remained in use, together with members of Classes 97 and 197 on the rack-operated Erzbergbahn, now allocated to just a handful of surviving steam sheds: Strasshof near Vienna (Classes 52, 77 and 93); Linz (Classes 77 and 52); Mistelbach, to the north of Vienna (Class 93); Gmünd (Class 93) and Vordernberg (Classes 97 and 197). In the following months, standard gauge steam operations declined relentlessly. On 23 May 1975 electric services commenced between Linz and Summerau, and a few days later Mistelbach shed closed with effect from the start of the summer timetable on 1 June. Steam-powered passenger services on the Erzbergbahn ended on 1 September, when the last diagram was turned over to railbuses.

On the narrow gauge, the ranks of steam locomotives were reduced by line closures, together with the advance of diesel traction, and by 1975 the ÖBB retained only 13 narrow gauge steam locomotives, belonging to four classes, which were allocated to Gmünd on the Waldviertelbahn, and to Garsten on the entirely steam operated Steyrtalbahn. In addition there were the 11 veteran metre gauge rack locomotives on the Schneeberg and Schafberg lines.

Away from the ÖBB, in spite of the continuing advance of diesel traction, steam could still be found on the Graz-Köflacher Bahn, which obtained its final second-hand ÖBB steam locomotives as late as 1972/73. In addition, it was still possible to see steam locomotives from eastern bloc countries at several border crossings. By 1975 steam had disappeared from regular scheduled services on the Steiermärkische Landesbahnen and the Zillertalbahn, although it retained a presence on their popular steam excursions. The Achenseebahn continued as before, with services in the hands of three of the original locomotives dating from 1889.

On the industrial systems also, working steam declined rapidly in the early 1970s, but clung on quietly and unobtrusively in a few remaining locations.

A memory of the rack-operated Erzbergbahn from Vordernberg to Eisenerz. The deserted streets of Vordernberg echo to the sound of an ÖBB Class 97 climbing above the town on 27 February 1974, raising an impressive exhaust in the still winter air. 18 months later, the final timetabled steam-powered passenger train would operate on the Erzbergbahn. *Author's Collection*

Standard Gauge Steam

1. Vienna (Wien)

The capital of Austria, Vienna is by far its largest city, and the central point of the major railway routes – as befits its previous role as the centre of the Austro-Hungarian empire – which link the largest cities of the present day Austrian republic, and connect Austria with its neighbours.

Although by the 1960s the primary rail routes to Vienna, the Westbahn and the Südbahn, were operated by either diesel or electric traction, steam survived into the 1970s at Wien Ost and Wien Nord depots, as well as Stadlau and Strasshof sheds. Particularly notable are the operation of Class 77 until 1974, and of Class 78 between 1970 and 1973, on the Nordbahn from Praterstern to Hohenau and Bernhardsthal, and the Nordwestbahn to Hollabrunn and Retz.

Vienna was the home of two major locomotive builders: the *Maschinen-Fabrik in Wien der privilegirten österreichisch-ungarischen Staats-Eisenbahn-Gesellschaft* (StEG), which ceased operations in 1930, and the *Lokomotivfabrik Floridsdorf* – often simply referred as Floridsdorf, but also sometimes as *Wiener Lokomotivfabrik Floridsdorf* (WLF), and as LOFAG (*Lokomotivfabrik Floridsdorf AG*), which supplied the last new steam locomotives to the ÖBB (17 members of Class 42) between 1945 and 1947, and delivered its last (electric) locomotives to the ÖBB in September 1969.

Above: Nos 52.7594 (Floridsdorf 16942 of 1944), 52.7596 (Floridsdorf 16944 of 1944) and 57.259 stand at Wien Ost depot on 8 September 1958. The two Class 52s were contemporaneous products of the Lokomotivfabrik Floridsdorf works, and both would survive until the end of regular ÖBB steam traction. *John McCann/Online Transport Archive*

Right: Seen at Wien Ost depot on 8 September 1958, No 77.10 (StEG 4286/1918), was the former kkStB No 629.25. It was withdrawn 10 years later, on 22 September 1968, after 50 years of service. *John McCann/Online Transport Archive*

Also present at Wien Ost shed on 8 September 1958 was superheated 0-10-0 No 57.259 (StEG 4195/1917), the former kkStB No 80.2902, which would be withdrawn two years later on 25. September 1960. *John McCann/Online Transport Archive*

No 78.624 (Floridsdorf 3158/1938), seen at Wien Franz-Josefs-Bahnhof depot on 8 May 1959, was one of an additional series of 10 Class 78 locomotives supplied to the Deutsche Reichsbahn in 1938. All members of Class 78 were equipped with Giesl ejectors and smoke deflectors in the 1950s. *Charles Firminger/Online Transport Archive*

No 3071.18 (Floridsdorf 3140/1937), originally numbered DT 1.18, stands at Wien Nordwestbahnhof depot on 8 May 1959. Officially classified as a steam railcar (*Dampftriebwagen*), Class 3071 was in reality a steam locomotive fitted with a luggage compartment. Of the 18 examples incorporated into the new ÖBB number scheme in 1953, all were withdrawn in 1967/68, with the exception of No 3071.09, which had already been taken out of service in February 1959. No 3071.18 was one of 10 which were officially withdrawn on 11 May 1968. *Charles Firminger/ Online Transport Archive*

Nos 77.22 (StEG 4387/1922) and 52.6407 (Schwartzkopff 12960/1944) await their next duties at Wien Nord depot on 3 September 1972. No 77.22 was one of 10 members of Class 77 which were transferred to the Hungarian State Railways (MÁV) in April 1945, but which returned to Austria in May/June 1950. Withdrawal came on 26 July 1973. No 52.6407 was withdrawn on 12 November 1975. *Author's Collection*

2. Niederösterreich

Niederösterreich (Lower Austria), in the north-east of Austria, is the country's largest state. It borders today's Czech Republic in the north, and Slovakia in the east, which together formed Czechoslovakia during the period covered by this book. It is bordered by Oberösterreich (Upper Austria) to the west, Steiermark (Styria) to the south, and Burgenland to the south-east. Niederösterreich consists of four regions with distinct characters – the Weinviertel (in the north-east), the Industrieviertel (in the south-east), the Mostviertel (in the west) and the Waldviertel (in the north-west). Although each of these four regions retains its own distinct identity, they no longer have any official significance.

Niederösterreich includes the railway centres of St Pölten (with its ÖBB works), Wiener Neustadt, Amstetten, St Valentin, Mistelbach, Krems an der Donau and Gmünd.

On 17 June 1967, a Class 52 locomotive passes a vineyard with a freight service on the Kamptal line between Krems and Horn, in a region known for its wine production. *Author's Collection*

2.1 The Industrieviertel

The Industrieviertel has borders with Vienna and the Weinviertel to the north, with the Mostviertel to the west, with Steiermark to the south, and with Burgenland to the east. The Vienna Woods (*Wienerwald*) forested highland region, at the north-east end of the Alps, forms a natural border to the west.

Despite its name, parts of the region in fact have a very rural character, and the Industrieviertel includes the Schneeberg – Niederösterreich's highest mountain at 2,076m. The communities in the area near the Schneeberg, including the town of Puchberg am Schneeberg, have been popular leisure destinations since the 18th century, and are known as the Schneebergland. This popularity grew with the arrival of the railway in April 1897.

No 93.1409 (StEG 4833/1928) is seen near Grünbach with a train from Wiener Neustadt to Puchberg am Schneeberg in September 1964. In the course of its climb into the mountains, the Puchberg branch features gradients of up to 4.4% (1 in 22). The average gradient for the 10km between Winzendorf and Grünbach is 2.2% (1 in 44), and some 3.6% (1 in 28) for the 3.4km from Grünbach to the summit at Grünbacher Sattel. *Marc Dahlström*

2.2 The Mostviertel

The northern boundary to the Mostviertel is formed by the Danube; it borders Steiermark to the south, and Oberösterreich to the west. The name Mostviertel derives from an important and popular product of the region – its perry and cider drinks. The economy of the Mostviertel was also long dominated by the iron & steel industry.

The Mostviertel region includes St Pölten, largest city and capital of Niederösterreich, as well as being a major railway centre, and Amstetten, an important railway town and junction of the line to Kleinreifling.

Above: No 77.08 (StEG 4284/1918) is seen at St Pölten on the evening of 12 April 1966 with train No 5616, the 5.20pm to Wien Südbahnhof via Hainfeld. Steam traction on this line, the *Niederösterreichische Südwestbahn*, ended four years later on 30 May 1970. *Charles Firminger/Online Transport Archive*

Opposite above: Probably having been cleaned for a special working, No 77.14 (StEG 4379/1922) is seen running light engine at St Pölten in 1969. No 77.14 was withdrawn just three years later on 22 November 1972 in its 50th year of service. *Author's Collection*

Opposite below: No 78.622 (Floridsdorf 3156/1938), seen at Amstetten shed in 1969, would be condemned the following year, on 1 August 1970. Amstetten's Class 78s were all withdrawn between 1968 and 1970. Behind No 78.622 is a member of Class 92, which has been coupled to a rigid framed tender from a Class 52 to extend its operational range for use on engineering trains during electrification work between Amstetten and Kleinreifling. *Author's Collection*

The Erlauftalbahn Pöchlarn – Scheibbs – Kienberg-Gaming

The 37.5km long Erlauftalbahn from Pöchlarn, on the Westbahn, to Kienberg-Gaming opened in 1877. For almost its complete length the line followed the course of the river Erlauf, a tributary of the Danube, into which it flows at Pöchlarn.

For almost 20 years the Erlauftalbahn was the domain of the distinctive ÖBB Class 770, a superheated 2-4-0T, of which 97 examples were built by Krauss, München between 1909 and 1916 as Class Pt 2/3 of the Königlich Bayerische Staatsbahn in Germany. Its design was remarkable for the exceptionally large distance between the pony truck and the front driving wheels. After World War 2, four examples

of the class – Nos 770.86, 92, 95 and 96 – were located in Austria, at Innsbruck and Wörgl. From December 1948 they were allocated to St Pölten, and used primarily on the Erlauftalbahn, where they proved to be highly successful. No 770.86 was withdrawn in 1968 as the last operational example of Class 770.

No 770.95 (Krauss, München 7023/1916) heads train No PG 19, the 2.05pm from Pöchlarn to Kienberg-Gaming, at Scheibbs (departure time 3.11pm) on 10 April 1966. *Charles Firminger/ Online Transport Archive*

Above: No 770.95 has arrived at Kienberg-Gaming, and has run light off its train. It will take water beside the locomotive shed, and be turned on the adjacent small turntable for the return journey to Pöchlarn. *Charles Firminger/ Online Transport Archive*

Right: Later on 10 April 1966, No 770.95 stands at Kienberg-Gaming with train No PG 22, the 4.6pm to Pöchlarn. Class 770s almost always ran chimney first, as their maximum permitted speed in this direction was 65km/h, but only 30km/h when running in reverse. The Erlauftalbahn, with a turntable at the terminus station at Kienberg-Gaming, was thus the ideal line for these locomotives. *Charles Firminger/ Online Transport Archive*

Left: No 770.95 stands at Wieselburg (departure 5.13pm) with train No PG 22, the 4.6pm from Kienberg-Gaming to Pöchlarn. *Charles Firminger/Online Transport Archive*

Below: No 93.1324 (Floridsdorf 2927/1927) stands at Neustift (28.7km from Pöchlarn) on 12 April 1966 with a goods train from Pöchlarn to Kienberg-Gaming. *Charles Firminger/Online Transport Archive*

Above: A little later, No 93.1324 leaves Neustift with its goods train and continues its journey. Withdrawal for No 93.1324 would come on 26 July 1973. *Charles Firminger/Online Transport Archive*

Right: Later on 12 April 1966 No 93.1324 is seen shunting at Neubruck with the goods train for Kienberg-Gaming. There are now just seven kilometres to go until it arrives at the terminus of the Erlauftalbahn at Kienberg-Gaming. *Charles Firminger/ Online Transport Archive*

Right: No 93.1467 (Floridsdorf 3036/1931) coasts along near Neustift on 12 April 1966 with train PG 18, the 12.5pm from Kienberg-Gaming to Pöchlarn. No 93.1467 (formerly No 378.167), the last-built member of the '378' series of 1931, would not be withdrawn until October 1975. *Charles Firminger/Online Transport Archive*

Below: Train No PG 20, the 2.20pm from Kienberg-Gaming to Pöchlarn arrives at Neustift on 12 April 1966 behind No 770.95. *Charles Firminger/Online Transport Archive*

Right: No 770.95 stands at Wieselburg an der Erlauf (departure time 3.28pm) with the 2.20pm from Kienberg-Gaming to Pöchlarn. Visible behind No 770.95 is a train on the narrow gauge line from Obergrafendorf to Gresten (known locally as *Die Krumpe*), which crossed the Erlauftalbahn at Wieselburg. *Charles Firminger/ Online Transport Archive*

Below: On 13 June 1968, No 93.1429 (Floridsdorf 2989/1928) has travelled 18km with train No PG 20, the 2.37pm from Kienberg-Gaming to Pöchlarn, and arrived at the well-kept station at Purgstall. Withdrawal for No 93.1429 would come eight years later on 16 August 1976. *Charles Firminger/Online Transport Archive*

2.3 The Waldviertel

Between the Danube to the south, the border to the Czech Republic (formerly Czechoslovakia) to the north, and the Weinviertel to the east, lies the Waldviertel – an attractive and predominantly rural part of Niederösterreich, which is characterised by agriculture, the forests which give the region its name, and in places also by large granite outcrops and small lakes.

The principal railway artery through the Waldviertel is the Franz-Josefs-Bahn from Wien (FJB) to Gmünd NÖ (161.9km), border station with the Czech Republic, continuing from there to Prague. At Sigmundsherberg (88.6km from Vienna), roughly half distance between Vienna and Gmünd, and junction for the Kamptalbahn to Hadersdorf am Kamp, there was a locomotive depot, complete with turntable. By 1905 the Franz-Josefs-Bahn was upgraded to double track, but the second track was removed between Sigmundsherberg and Gmünd in 1959, and then between Absdorf-Hippersdorf (44km) and Sigmundsherberg in 1967. The centre of operations in the Waldviertel was to be found at the station, the adjacent goods yard, and the locomotive shed at Schwarzenau (138.2km), from where branch lines led in a northerly direction to Waidhofen an der Thaya and Fratres, and to Zwettl and Martinsberg-Gutenbrunn to the south. A further branch ran north from Göpfritz to Raabs.

In the early 1970s the Waldviertel, where the last examples of Class 93 were based at Gmünd until the end of steam operations, was one of the final strongholds of steam traction.

Opposite above: No 95.108 (Wiener Neustadt 5640/1922) stands at Sigmundsherberg shed on 1 September 1963. Almost all members of Class 95 were withdrawn between 1968 and 1970; No 95.108 together with six of its classmates on 12 April 1968. *Author's Collection*

Opposite below: Also present at Sigmundsherberg shed on 1 September 1963 was No 292.2101 (Henschel 14663/1917). During World War 1 the Austrian military railways (*k.u.k. Heeresbahn*) placed an order for 22 0-8-0Ts (as Class 578) from Henschel in Kassel, as the Austrian locomotive builders had full order books at the time. 12 examples remained with the BBÖ after the war, and following World War 2 eight were inherited by the ÖBB, which classified them as Class 292. Nos 292.2101 and 292.2105 were withdrawn on 5 December 1966 as the last members of the class. *Author's Collection*

Below: No 93.1411 (StEG 4835/1928) departs Schwarzenau on Monday 26 July 1971 with train No SM 87, the 3.15pm to Zwettl (timetabled arrival at 4.3pm). No 93.1411 survived for a further two years, and was not withdrawn from service until 28 September 1973. *Author's Collection*

Three Days in the Waldviertel – June 1968

Above: On Friday 14 June 1968, No 52.3520 (Krauss Maffei 16646/1943) stands at Horn with train No 5120, the 6.10am from Gars-Thunau to Sigmundsherberg. No 52.3520 would survive until the end of steam traction on the ÖBB, and was not officially withdrawn until 25 July 1977. The following year this once proud locomotive suffered the indignity of being converted to a snowplough.
Charles Firminger/Online Transport Archive

Above: In the late morning of 14 June 1968, No 52.478 (Borsig 15575/1943) leaves Schwarzenau with a goods train for Sigmundsherberg. The Giesl ejector-equipped No 52.478 was eventually withdrawn on 20 October 1975. *Charles Firminger/ Online Transport Archive*

Right: On 14 June 1968, No 93.1415 (StEG 4839/1928) pauses at Waidhofen an der Thaya (arr. 12.53pm, dep. 1.41pm) with train No ZS 63, the 10.40am from Fratres to Schwarzenau, which was due to reach Schwarzenau at 2pm. *Charles Firminger/ Online Transport Archive*

Above: No 93.1303 (Floridsdorf 2906/1927) stands at the modest halt at Fratres on 14 June 1968 with train No ZS 21, the 2.40pm from Fratres to Schwarzenau. With the coming of the new border with Czechoslovakia, operations beyond here to Zlabings (today Slavonice), five kilometres distant, were terminated, and the tracks were removed. As a result, for many years the line from Schwarzenau terminated at Fratres. As this rudimentary terminus possessed neither run-round facilities nor even a siding, all trains had to be propelled either to or from Fratres. *Charles Firminger/ Online Transport Archive*

Opposite above: On 14 June 1968, No 93.1366 (StEG 4785/1927) stands at Gross Siegharts (dep. 5.53pm) with train No GR 67, the 5.35pm from Göpfritz to Raabs. *Charles Firminger/Online Transport Archive*

Opposite below: Having reached the terminus at Raabs an der Thaya (arr. 6.16pm) with the 5.35pm from Göpfritz, No 93.1366 has shunted its train, and stands in the late evening sun in front of the impressive station building at Raabs, ready to return south as train No GR 68, the 7pm from Raabs to Göpfritz. *Charles Firminger/ Online Transport Archive*

Opposite above: No 93.1407 (StEG 4831/1928) arrives at Bernschlag (5.6km from Schwarzenau) on 15 June 1968 with train No SM 39, the 6.1pm from Schwarzenau to Martinsberg-Gutenbrunn. The 58km journey to Martinsberg-Gutenbrunn was scheduled to take a total of one hour 55 minutes, with a timetabled arrival time of 7.56pm. *Charles Firminger/ Online Transport Archive*

Opposite below: On the evening of 15 June 1968, No 93.1318 (Floridsdorf 2921/1927) has arrived at Schwarzenau with the 2.50pm from Martinsberg-Gutenbrunn (arr. 5.40pm). No 93.1318 was withdrawn on 20 October 1972 after a working life of 45 years. *Charles Firminger/Online Transport Archive*

Below: No 93.1392 stands at Schwarzenau, having arrived with the 6.22pm from Waidhofen an der Thaya. Withdrawal for No 93.1392 would follow five years later, on 22 June 1973. *Charles Firminger/Online Transport Archive*

Above: No 93.1392 (StEG 4811/1927) arrives at Schwarzenau on the evening of 15 June 1968 with the 6.22pm mixed train from Waidhofen an der Thaya. *Charles Firminger/ Online Transport Archive*

Above: On Sunday 16 June 1968, the rather down-at-heel No 93.1415 (StEG 4839/1928) awaits departure from Schwarzenau with the 8.20am mixed train to Zwettl. Whilst the locomotive has disc driving wheels, both pony trucks are fitted with spoked wheels. No 93.1415 was another locomotive to be withdrawn on 22 June 1973. *Charles Firminger/Online Transport Archive*

Opposite above: Class 93 No 93.1364 (StEG 4783/1927) arrives at Schwarzenau with a train from Fratres on 7 April 1972. *Chris Gammell*

Opposite below: Also on 7 April 1972, No 93.1390 (StEG 4809/1927) is seen departing Schwarzenau with a train for Martinsberg-Gutenbrunn. No 93.1390 would be withdrawn on 14 March 1975. *Chris Gammell*

April 1972

The Czechoslovak State Railways, ČSD, were responsible for services between the border stations of Gmünd NÖ and České Velenice. The regular locomotive in the 1970s was the always well turned-out No 556.0506 (Škoda 3531/1958) of the ČSD. Class 556 was a highly successful 2-10-0 design, of which a total of 510 examples were built by Skoda between 1951 and 1958, and which remained in operation until the end of steam traction on the ČSD. No 556.0506 leaves Gmünd station in April 1972 with a goods train for České Velenice. *Author's Collection*

2.4 The Weinviertel

The Weinviertel, situated in the north-east corner of Austria, borders the present day Czech Republic to the north and Slovakia to the east, which between them constituted the country of Czechoslovakia during the period covered by this book. Within Austria it borders the other three regions of Niederösterreich – the Industrieviertel to the south, the Mostviertel to the south-west, and the Waldviertel to the west. The largest city of the Weinviertel is Stockerau, approximately 30km north-west of Vienna. As its name indicates, the Weinviertel is the most important wine producing region of Austria.

Significant locations in the last years of steam included Mistelbach, Groß Schweinbarth, Laa an der Thaya, Gänserndorf, Hohenau and Dobermannsdorf. The most important operational centre of the extensive rail network in the Weinviertel, until 1975 Mistelbach possessed a busy locomotive depot, where Class 93 locomotives dominated until the end of steam operations. A further significant centre was Groß Schweinbarth, meeting point of lines running via Pirawarth to Mistelbach and Dobermannsdorf in a northerly direction, and to Gänserndorf and Stammersdorf to the south.

A Class 77 4-6-2T is seen near Stockerau in September 1964 at the head of a train of modernised four-wheel coaches, fitted with steel bodies in the 1950s. *Marc Dahlström*

Above: Class 93 No 93.1464 (Floridsdorf 3033/1931), seen at Mistelbach depot in September 1974, would survive until the end of standard gauge steam operations on the ÖBB except for the Erzbergbahn. *Author's Collection*

Opposite above: Two years earlier, the well turned-out No 93.1464, originally BBÖ No 378.164, stands at Mistelbach Lokalbahnhof on the line from Korneuburg to Hohenau in the summer of 1972. *Author's Collection*

Opposite below: Nos 93.1322 (Floridsdorf 2925/1927) and 93.1368 (StEG 4787/27) pause at Hohenruppersdorf, between Zistersdorf and Pirawarth, on 27 February 1975 with train No 7415, the 2.9pm from Hohenau and 2.34pm departure from Dobermannsdorf, to Stammersdorf (arr. 4.58pm). *Author's Collection*

3. Oberösterreich

Oberösterreich (Upper Austria), the country's fourth largest state, borders Bavaria to the north-west, the Czech Republic to the north, Niederösterreich to the east, Steiermark to the south, and Salzburg to the south-east. Situated on the Danube, Linz, the capital city of Oberösterreich, is Austria's third largest city. Linz is located on the Westbahn between Vienna and Salzburg, and is a major railway centre, the site of a large railway works and an important locomotive depot. The Pyhrnbahn runs south from Linz to Selzthal, and the Summerauer Bahn runs north to Summerau on the border with the Czech Republic (part of the former Czechoslovakia).

Other important railway centres include Attnang-Puchheim (starting point of the Salzkammergut line to Stainach-Irdning), Wels (junction for Passau) and Vöcklabruck.

Below: Class 50 2-10-0 No 50.2835 (Krauss Maffei 16352/1942) stands on the turntable at Linz shed on the sunny 7 September 1958, It would be withdrawn 10 years later on 20 November 1968. By 1950 just a dozen members of Class 50 remained in service with the ÖBB, all of which were allocated to Linz and often used on heavy ore trains between Eisenerz and Linz. *John McCann/ Online Transport Archive*

Opposite above: No 52.6966 (Floridsdorf 16419/1943), fitted with a conventional blastpipe and without smoke deflectors, is also seen on the turntable at Linz on 7 September 1958. The Class 52 would remain in traffic for a further 16 years, eventually being withdrawn on 4 November 1974. *John McCann/Online Transport Archive*

Opposite below: Giesl ejector fitted Class 93 No 93.1310 (Floridsdorf 2913/1927), basking in the sunshine at Linz depot on 7 September 1958, would survive almost to the end of ÖBB steam, not being withdrawn from service until 4 June 1976. *John McCann/Online Transport Archive*

Above: At the beginning of the 1950s more than 30 veteran 0-8-0 Class 55 locomotives remained in service, but seven examples were taken out of traffic as early as August 1952. For most of the remaining examples the end would come between 1958 and 1961. No 55.5721 (StEG 2686/1898), seen at Linz depot on 7 September 1958, would be withdrawn less than a year later on 5 August 1959. *John McCann/Online Transport Archive*

Opposite above: Class 77 No 77.15 (StEG 4380/1922) stands at Garsten with a well-occupied train heading for Kleinreifling in 1965. Built as BBÖ No 629.30, No 77.15 would eventually be withdrawn on 20 October 1972. *Author's Collection*

Opposite below: No 152.194 (Schwartzkopff 12199/1943) awaits departure from Garsten in 1965 with a goods train for St Valentin. The 37 members of Class 52 fitted with bar frames which entered ÖBB stock after the war became ÖBB Class 152. No 152.194 (originally DRB No 52 194) was withdrawn in October 1972. *Author's Collection*

Above: In August 1960, No 93.1428 (Floridsdorf 2988/1928) awaits departure time at the picturesque station of Gmunden Seebahnhof with a train to Lambach, located on the Westbahn between Attnang-Puchheim and Wels. In the background the rails end at the edge of the Traunsee lake. No 93.1428 was withdrawn from ÖBB service in March 1970. *Phil Tatt/Online Transport Archive*

Opposite above: No 50.1171 (Skoda 1250/1942) stands ready for its next duty at Linz on 26 July 1970. The large 'Wagner' style smoke deflectors give No 50.1171 an impressive appearance. Two years later, in August 1972, No 50.1171 was acquired from the ÖBB by the Graz-Köflacher Bahn, where it would remain active for several years longer. *Author's Collection*

Opposite below: No 52.7061 (Floridsdorf 16514/1943) leaves Summerau, border station with Czechoslovakia, with a freight train heading towards Freistadt on 7 June 1971. The hilly countryside of the upper *Mühlviertel* region resulted in a winding route to Summerau. Steam operations on the line from Linz to Freistadt and Summerau ended on 31 May 1975 with the commencement of electric services. *Author's Collection*

4. Salzburg

Salzburg, which lies on the river Salzach, is Austria's fourth largest city, and capital of the state of the same name, which borders Oberösterreich to the north-east, Steiermark to the south, Kärnten (Carinthia) to the south, the Tyrol to the south-west, and Bavaria to the north.

Salzburg lies at the end of the Westbahn from Vienna via Linz. From Salzburg the Westbahn (Salzburg-Tiroler-Bahn) continues to the west via Bischofshofen to Innsbruck, and from Schwarzach-St Veit the Tauernbahn runs south to Villach. Salzburg is also the junction for the line which crosses the border into Germany, via Freilassing and Rosenheim to Munich.

Below: The ÖBB inherited 10 members of the USA Transportation Corps 0-6-0T shunting locomotive of Class S100, which became ÖBB Class 989. They were divided into sub-classes according to their builder, as ÖBB Nos 989.01-05 (Vulcan), 989.101-103 (Davenport) and 989.201-202 (Porter). The first two were withdrawn by ÖBB in 1963, and the remainder in February/March 1968. On 7 September 1958, No 989.04 (Vulcan Iron Works 4539/1945), formerly USA TC No 6169, stands on the turntable of its home depot at Salzburg. Although it was one of the last-built members of Class S100, No 989.04 was the first example of ÖBB Class 989 to be withdrawn, on 20 March 1963. *John McCann/Online Transport Archive*

Above: On 7 September 1958, No 91.61 (Krauss, Linz 5591/1906) stands at Salzburg depot. In 1953 a total of 15 members of the former Class 99 and nine examples of the Class 199 development of the design were incorporated in the new ÖBB number scheme of that year, as Classes 91 and 91.1 respectively. By 1968 all but three members of the two classes had been taken out of service. One of the victims of this withdrawal process was No 91.61, which succumbed on 20 January 1963. *John McCann/Online Transport Archive*

Right: A large number of members of the former KPEV Class G10 remained in Austria as Class 657 following World War 2, being withdrawn progressively by the ÖBB in the 1950s and 1960s. Amongst these robust freight locomotives was No 657.2295 (Borsig 10794/1921), which is seen outside the shed at its home depot of Salzburg on 7 September 1958. No 657.2295 was withdrawn on 5 July 1965. *John McCann/Online Transport Archive*

Above: No 01082, seen on 7 September 1958 at its home depot of Salzburg, was formerly ÖBB No 175.803 (Böhmisch-Mährische Maschinenfabrik 417/1912), which had been converted into a mobile locomotive washing-out unit in April 1957. 36 examples of kkStB Class 29, a superheated compound 2-6-2T, intended for passenger services, had been built in 1936. 16 members of the class became ÖBB Class 175 following World War 2, but all had been withdrawn by September 1962. For No 01082 the end finally came on 15 January 1962, 50 years after its construction. *John McCann/Online Transport Archive*

Opposite: No 93.1450 (Krauss, Linz 1500/1929) arrives at Zeltweg with a passenger train on 7 May 1959. Although some 109 members of Class 93 were still in service with the ÖBB on 1 January 1970, No 93.1450 would be withdrawn on 1 August of that year. *Charles Firminger/Online Transport Archive*

5. Obersteiermark

Steiermark (Styria), situated in the centre and south of Austria, is the second largest and most heavily wooded Austrian state. Obersteiermark (Upper Styria), the mountainous, northern part of Steiermark, is largely rural in character, with the exception of the industrial region between Judenburg and Mürzzuschlag in the valley of the rivers Mur and Mürz, location of the large steelworks at Donawitz, near Leoben.

The Obersteiermark region includes the important railway centre of Selzthal, situated on the Pyhrnbahn from Linz, the Ennstalbahn between Kleinreifling and Bischofshofen, and the Rudolfsbahn to St Michael. In steam days it was notable for including the railway centres of Hieflau, Leoben, Bruck an der Mur and Knittelfeld – location of the ÖBB works responsible for the maintenance of the ÖBB's last steam locomotives.

During the period covered by this book, iron ore was transported in enormous quantities from the Erzberg (Iron Mountain) not only to the ÖAMG blast furnaces at Donawitz, but also the VÖEST steelworks at Linz. Into the 1970s the juxtaposition of dramatic scenery and heavy industry attracted many railway enthusiasts to the Obersteiermark region – in particular to Selzthal, Hieflau, Eisenerz, and above all to Vordernberg for the daily spectacle of steam operations on the rack equipped Erzbergbahn.

Left: No 35.212 (BMMF 487/1913) is seen at Bruck an der Mur depot on 22 May 1964. A superheated two-cylinder compound, originally built as kkStB No 429.924, it was rebuilt by the BBÖ in the 1930s with Lentz poppet valves. More recently, No 35.212 has additionally been fitted with air brakes, electric lighting and a Giesl ejector. *Charles Firminger/Online Transport Archive*

Below: No 57.268 (Wiener Neustadt 5550/1920) stands on the turntable at Bruck an der Mur shed on 22 May 1964. The members of Class 57 were progressively taken out of service during the 1950s and 1960s, but the tenacious No 57.268, carrying a rather incongruous Giesl ejector, lasted almost a further four years, and was finally withdrawn on 7 March 1968 as one of the last working examples of the class. *Charles Firminger/Online Transport Archive*

Right: No 392.2532 (Wiener Neustadt 5803/1927) is seen at Bruck an der Mur on 22 May 1964. Three years later it would be converted to steam heating unit No 01081[II] in December 1967. Final withdrawal would follow in 1970. *Charles Firminger/Online Transport Archive*

Below: No 95.111 is engaged in shunting empty stock at Vordernberg on 22 May 1964. 20 examples of BBÖ Class 82, an impressive 2-10-2T locomotive, entered service in 1922, followed by a further four in 1928. They were used especially on steeply graded lines, where they proved to be highly successful. 22 examples would become ÖBB Class 95 after World War 2. All were withdrawn between 1968 and 1970, with the exception of No 95.113, condemned in September 1972 as the last of the class. For No 95.111 the end came on 12 April 1968. *Charles Firminger/Online Transport Archive*

Above: On 22 May 1964, Class 97 No 97.204 (Floridsdorf 735/1890), hauling two open wagons loaded with timber, drifts past the locomotive shed at Eisenerz, where Class 86 No 86.751 (MBA 13766/1942) is being prepared for its next duty. Next to No 86.751 stands another member of Class 97. *Charles Firminger/ Online Transport Archive*

Right: A little later on the same day, No 86.751 collects the stock to form train No 5035, the 3.42pm to Hieflau, from a siding beside the locomotive shed at Eisenerz. *Charles Firminger/ Online Transport Archive*

Above: Nos 86.751 and 86.106 leave the yard at Hieflau on 22 May 1964 with a goods train including three rebodied *Spantenwagen* four-wheel coaches. For many years, the Obersteiermark region was a stronghold of these powerful 2-8-2Ts, which were often to be seen hauling heavy iron ore trains in tandem with 2-10-0s of Class 52. *Charles Firminger/ Online Transport Archive*

Right: On the evening of 22 May 1964, No 78.619 (Floridsdorf 3153/1938) leaves Hieflau with a train from Amstetten to Bischofshofen, which it will haul as far as Selzthal. *Charles Firminger/Online Transport Archive*

Selzthal

The town of Selzthal situated in the heart of Austria, was an important railway centre, the site of a busy locomotive depot with a semi-roundhouse, and of an extensive freight yard. Selzthal was the meeting point of lines to Linz (the Pyhrnbahn), via Hieflau to Kleinreifling (the Ennstalbahn) and Eisenerz, to Stainach-Irdning and Bischofshofen (the Ennstalbahn once again), and via the Schoberpass line to St Michael, on the line from Leoben to Villach and Klagenfurt.

Above: Giesl ejector fitted No 52.3816 (Floridsdorf 17305/1944) pauses with a train of ore wagons opposite Selzthal station, with its distinctive platform canopies, on 24 July 1958. No 52.3816 would survive until the final days of ÖBB main line steam. *Author's Collection*

Opposite above: On the evening of 22 May 1964, No 78.619 passes Selzthal station on its way light engine to the shed. Withdrawal for No 78.619 would come six years later on 1 August 1970. *Charles Firminger/Online Transport Archive*

Opposite below: Also on the evening of 22 May 1964, No 35.212, delivered in 1913 as kkStB No 429.924, stands opposite the signalbox at Selzthal. No 35.212 had a long and successful career, finally being withdrawn on 5 December 1966 together with most of the other remaining members of Class 35. *Charles Firminger/ Online Transport Archive*

Right: No 35.205 (Floridsdorf 2112/1913) of Bruck an der Mur shed stands at Leoben Hauptbahnhof in February 1963. Already some 50 years old, No 35.205 remained in ÖBB service for a further two years before finally being withdrawn on 5 July 1965. *Marc Dahlström*

Below: No 52.844 (Krenau 1465/1944) is seen at Gstatterboden, on the highly scenic *Gesäusestrecke* between Hieflau and Selzthal, at the head of a lengthy goods train on 16 April 1966. *Charles Firminger/Online Transport Archive*

Mürzzuschlag – Neuberg

In the days of steam traction, Mürzzuschlag was an important intermediate station on the Südbahn route, responsible for providing locomotives for piloting and banking duties on the famous Semmering line. In 1879, an 11.5km branch line was opened from Mürzzuschlag along the Mürz valley to Neuberg an der Mürz, which received considerable freight traffic from a sawmill at Neuberg. In the final years of ÖBB steam operations the line became well known amongst enthusiasts as the last stamping ground of the veteran compound 2-6-0Ts of Classes 91 and 91.1, originally built from 1897 as kkStB Class 99, and developed from 1908 with increased water and coal capacity as Class 199. The ÖBB classified the former Class 99

locomotives as Class 91, and the members of Class 199 as Class 91.1. In the 1960s the number of survivors of both classes decreased steadily, and by 1969 there were just three examples left in service at Mürzzuschlag – Nos 91.44, 91.107 and 91.109. These were finally withdrawn in 1972, with the dieselisation of services between Mürzzuschlag and Neuberg.

A 1963 view of No 91.74 (Krauss, Linz 5822/1907) waiting to depart Mürzzuschlag with a train for Neuberg. No 91.74 would be withdrawn in January 1968. *Author's Collection*

On Wednesday 13 April 1966, No 91.107 (Krauss, Linz 6025/1908) hurries train No MN 23, the 1.56pm from Mürzzuschlag to Neuberg along the Mürz valley near Kapellen. Arrival at Neuberg is due at 2.25pm. *Charles Firminger/Online Transport Archive*

In another view on the sunny 13 April 1966, No 91.32 (Krauss, Linz 4267/1900) departs Kapellen after shunting mixed train No MN 93, the 2.35pm from Mürzzuschlag to Neuberg. Although the Neuberg branch was just 11.5km long, the timetabled journey time for train No MN 93 was no less than 61 minutes, with an arrival time at Neuberg of 3.36pm. No 91.32 would be withdrawn three and half years later on 5 October 1969, after a working life of 69 years. *Charles Firminger/Online Transport Archive*

Above: No 91.107 stands with its train at Neuberg in a late 1960s view, which illustrates the picturesque scenery of the Mürz valley at Neuberg. *Author's Collection*

Right: The driver and fireman of No 91.107 patiently await departure time at Neuberg on a rainy day in 1971. *Author's Collection*

6. The Erzbergbahn

The Erzbergbahn, a remarkable 19.7km long standard gauge rack line, located at the eastern end of the Austrian Alps, was built to transport iron ore from the famous 'Iron Mountain' – the *Erzberg*. Opened in 1891, the Erzbergbahn connected Vordernberg at its southern end with Eisenerz, via the Präbichl pass. At Vordernberg it connected with the line from Leoben, which ran past the enormous blast furnaces at Donawitz, and at Eisenerz it met the line from Hieflau. The rack section started immediately on departing Vordernberg (768m), and the line climbed 436 metres to the summit at Präbichl (1,204m), a distance of 7.7km, at an average gradient of 5.7% (1 in 17.5). In the opposite direction the line gained 512m over a distance of 12km between Eisenerz (692m) and Präbichl, at an average gradient of 4.3% (1 in 23.2). The incline varied repeatedly; intermediate stations had only very gentle gradients and were without rack rails, but the steepest sections reached a gradient of 7.1% (I in 14). Between Vordernberg and Eisenerz the 19.7km route featured six viaducts and five tunnels.

The first locomotives on the line were 0-6-2T rack tanks of kkStB Class 69, delivered from 1890 onwards, with a total of no fewer than 18 examples being built, with modifications, between then and 1908. Two were transferred to Germany in 1944, and did not return to Vordernberg. In 1956 a further two were sold to Hungary. The remaining 14 locomotives, as ÖBB Class 97, would bear the brunt of

duties on the 'Iron Mountain' until the end of steam traction in September 1978.

The search for more powerful locomotives led in 1912 to the construction of three 0-12-0T rack tanks – kkStB Class 269, which would later become ÖBB Class 197. Although successful – with the first withdrawal not coming until 1975, and the last member of the class remaining in service until the end of steam traction on the 'Iron Mountain' – only three examples were built.

The need for even more powerful locomotives to increase iron ore production from the Erzberg to support the war effort, led to the development of two enormous 2-12-2T rack tanks (later ÖBB Class 297), notable as being the largest steam rack locomotives in the world. These giants were not very successful, being prone to mechanical failure, and also exhibiting a tendency to damage the tracks. Because of their considerable weight, their use was limited to the southern section of the line between Vordernberg and Präbichl. Both locomotives were out of use as early as 1964.

The Erzbergbahn in winter. In January 1962, a Class 97 locomotive propels its passenger train heading for Präbichl on the northern section of the Erzbergbahn near Feistawiese, leaving a fine exhaust trail in the still, cold air. *Marc Dahlström*

No 97.204 (Floridsdorf 735/1890) stands at Eisenerz, at the northern end of the 19.7km rack operated Erzbergbahn in September 1963. From Eisenerz a conventional line leads to Hieflau. To the left in the background can be seen Eisenerz locomotive shed, and beyond looms the mighty Erzberg, its upper reaches disappearing in the clouds. *Author's Collection*

Above: In another September 1963 scene, colossal 2-12-2T No 297.401 (Floridsdorf 9100/1941) stands on the turntable at Vordernberg shed, where all of the ÖBB's Class 97, 197 and 297 locomotives were allocated. *Author's Collection*

Below: Class 197 No 197.301 (Floridsdorf 2090/1912), originally kkStB No 269.01, stands on the turntable at its home depot of Vordernberg in the 1960s. The three members of Class 197 had 12 driving wheels and two separately driven rack wheels. The ÖBB fitted all three with Giesl ejectors in the 1950s. No 197.301 would remain in service, as the last active member of its class, until the end of steam traction in 1978. *Author's Collection*

Right: No 97.203 (Floridsdorf 734/1890) stands at Glaslbremse, between Vordernberg Markt and Präbichl, with train No 5005, the 12.05pm from Leoben to Eisenerz, the 12.59pm departure from Vordernberg, on 22 May 1964. No 97.203 replenishes its water reserves whilst the train waits to cross train No 5004, the 11.40am from Hieflau to Leoben. As can be seen, there was no central rack rail at stations.
Charles Firminger/Online Transport Archive

Below: Nos 97.205 (Floridsdorf 817/1892) and 97.201 (Floridsdorf 732/1890) set off from Vordernberg on 14 April 1966 with a train of empties. No 97.205 was withdrawn on 29 November 1977, but No 97.201, originally kkStB No 6901, would continue in service until the end of steam operations the following year.
Charles Firminger/Online Transport Archive

No 297.401 is seen stored out of use at Vordernberg on 14 April 1966. Less successful than their predecessors of Classes 97 and 197, the two members of Class 297 had short working lives, although both were fitted with Giesl ejectors. No 297.402 was taken out of use in the 1950s and used as a spare parts donor for its classmate, but No 297.401 lasted in traffic only until 1964, with official withdrawal following in April 1968. *Charles Firminger/Online Transport Archive*

No 97.208 (Floridsdorf 820/1892) stands at Vordernberg Markt with a passenger service. Vordernberg Markt station was just 1.6km from Vordernberg station, but some 78m higher, with an average gradient between them of 4.9% (1 in 20.4). As well as the through services between Vordernberg and Eisenerz, there was also a local shuttle service between Vordernberg and Vordernberg Markt. *Author's Collection*

On a fine summer's day No 97.204 forges up the incline above the town of Vordernberg with a mixed rake of empty ore wagons. No 97.204 was one of the first series of the class, dating from 1890, which were delivered in advance of the start of services the following year, and was originally kkStB No 6904, later No 69.04. *Author's Collection*

A few moments later the first member of the class, No 97.201 (Floridsdorf 732/1890) appears, assisting at the rear of the train. Both locomotives have a conventional blastpipe and chimney. Rack drive is through two coupled toothed wheels, located between the first two coupled axles. *Author's Collection*

Snow still lies on the mountains on 3 March 1975, as Nos 97.205 (front) and 97.204 (rear) work together to lift a long train of empty ore wagons between Vordernberg (departing at 9.50am) and Vordernberg Markt. *Author's Collection*

Above: Nine days earlier, winter has not yet relented as Nos 97.201 and 97.205 approach with a rake of empties near Glaslbremse on 22 February 1975. *Author's Collection*

Right: On the same day, Nos 97.208 and 97.204 generate impressive exhausts as they climb slowly above Vordernberg with a long train of empty ore wagons. *Author's Collection*

7. Graz

Graz, the capital of the state of Steiermark (Styria) in the south-east of Austria, has a long history, and is the country's second largest city. It lies on the river Mur, roughly 200km south-west of Vienna. An important railway centre, Graz is connected to Vienna by the Südbahn via the famous Semmering line over the Alps, and is the headquarters of the independent standard gauge Graz-Köflacher Bahn.

The *Grazer Maschinen- und Waggonbau-Aktiengesellschaft*, which existed under the Graz name since the 1890s, was an important builder of narrow gauge rolling stock, and played a significant role in the development of both diesel and electric motive power. In 1941 the Graz company was merged with the Vienna-based Simmering and Paukerwerk firms, giving rise to the *Simmering-Graz-Pauker AG* (SGP). In the last months of the war in Europe, the SGP factory at Graz was almost completely destroyed by air-raids, but the business was rapidly re-established following the war.

Class 113, a powerful 4-8-0 tender locomotive, was developed for the BBÖ to address the need for locomotives capable of operating increasingly heavy trains on the Westbahn. A total of 40 members of the class were built between 1923 and 1928, of which 33 passed to the ÖBB after World War 2, becoming ÖBB Class 33. All members of Class 33 were withdrawn by the ÖBB during the 1960s, with No 33.130 (StEG 4739/1925), seen at Graz shed on 9 September 1958 succumbing on 21 October 1963.
John McCann/Online Transport Archive

Above: Imposing 2-10-0 No 42.2702 (Floridsdorf 17585/1945) is seen in steam at Graz shed on 9 September 1958. Although the newest examples had been built as recently as 1946/47, Class 42 soon became surplus to requirements, and a large number were sold to Hungary as scrap in 1957. Five were acquired by the

Hungarian Railways (MÁV) in late 1958/early 1959. Most of the remaining ÖBB Class 42 locomotives were taken out of service between 1963 and 1964 – amongst these No 42.2702 in August 1963. *John McCann/Online Transport Archive*

Right: Present at Graz shed on the same date was Giesl ejector equipped No 57.285 (StEG 4303/1919), together with Nos 42.2706 (Floridsdorf 17589/1946) and 77.73 (StEG 3944/1914). KkStB Class 80 was a 0-10-0 intended for use on freight services, which also found use with the Südbahn. The first examples were turned out as compounds, but from 1911 until 1918 it was built in large numbers in a simple expansion version. 60 examples became ÖBB Class 57, the last of which survived until 1968. For No 57.285 the end came five years earlier than this, with withdrawal taking place in June 1963. *John McCann/Online Transport Archive*

Opposite above: No 78.616 (Floridsdorf 3098/1936), formerly BBÖ No 729.16, standing outside the shed at its home depot of Graz on 21 May 1964, was the last of the 16 members of the class which were built for the BBÖ between 1931 and 1936. A further batch of 10 locomotives, incorporating a number of modifications, was supplied in 1938 to an order placed by the Deutsche Reichsbahn. *Charles Firminger/Online Transport Archive*

Opposite below: Despite its rather run-down appearance at Graz locomotive depot on 21 May 1964, No 77.35 (Krauss, Linz 1211/1921) would survive for another five years before being condemned on 10 October 1969. *Charles Firminger/Online Transport Archive*

Above: No 78.616 is seen at Graz locomotive depot again on 20 June 1967. All members of the class survived World War 2, and were equipped by the ÖBB in the 1950s with Giesl ejectors, together with superheater boost equipment. Following the withdrawal of the majority of its classmates between January 1968 and August 1970, No 78.616 was finally condemned on 26 July 1973 as one of the last members of Class 78. *Author's Collection*

8. The Graz-Köflacher Bahn

The Graz-Köflacher Bahn (GKB) was built to transport coal from the mines of the west Steiermark coalfield. The original 41km long main line from Graz, where it connected with the Südbahn, to Köflach, opened in 1860. A second line followed in 1873, running from Lieboch, on the original line to Köflach, to Wies-Eibiswald (51km). In 1907 the Sulmtalbahn was opened, running from Leibnitz, situated on the Südbahn main line to the south of Graz, to a junction with the Graz-Köflacher Bahn not far from Wies-Eibiswald. In April 1930, the Sulmtalbahn was merged with the GKB, and its services were integrated into the timetable of the GKB between Graz and Wies-Eibiswald. Services on the Sulmtalbahn ended in 1967.

The Graz-Köflacher Bahn became an increasingly popular destination for railway enthusiasts in the 1960s and 1970s, thanks to its long-standing policy of using locomotives obtained second-hand from the main line railway companies, which made it a mecca for devotees of vintage steam. In the 1960s there were ex-Südbahn Class 29 0-6-0s, dating from the 1860s and still in use 100 years later, together with Südbahn Class 17c 4-4-0s from the 1890s, and kkStB Class 30 2-6-2Ts which dated from 1900. During the 1950s these veteran locomotives were largely displaced by much larger and more powerful Class 56 2-8-0s, built by the kkStB in the second decade of the 20th century, which in turn were reinforced during the 1960s and early 1970s by even larger redundant ÖBB Class 50 and Class 152 locomotives. Even before the arrival of the big 2-10-0s, diesel traction had been introduced by the GKB from 1965 onwards, and the role of steam locomotives diminished steadily.

On the late afternoon of 9 September 1958, Graz-Köflacher Bahn No 680 (StEG 513/1860) stands outside the shed at Graz. Between 1860 and 1872 the Südbahn ordered more than 200 Class 29 locomotives. The GKB acquired no fewer than 18 members of the class between 1924 and 1926, but all but four of these had already been withdrawn by 1936. Despite their age, the surviving four locomotives – Nos 671, 674, 677 and 680 – remained in use until the start of the 1960s. No 680 was taken out of service in 1964, but in 1967 it was sold for preservation in Germany. *John McCann/Online Transport Archive*

Above: In another view on 9 September 1958, GKB No 372 (Floridsdorf 768/1891) waits at the shed for its next turn of duty. A total of 62 locomotives of Class 17c were built for the Südbahn, with deliveries continuing until 1901, but even at the time when members of the class were entering service, its design was already outdated, being a development of Class 17a dating back to 1882. In 1924 the GKB acquired eight examples from the BBÖ, which it used primarily on passenger services. *John McCann/ Online Transport Archive*

Left: On the evening of 9 September 1958, No 409 (Floridsdorf 1088/1897) stands at Graz in the late evening sun at the head of an empty stock formation. Although two members of Class 17c had been withdrawn by the GKB as early as 1927, the others were not retired from service until the 1950s and 1960s. *John McCann/Online Transport Archive*

Above: No 677 (StEG 510/1860) is seen on shunting duties at Graz in July 1961. *Phil Tatt/Online Transport Archive*

Opposite above: Class 17c No 406 (Wiener Neustadt 3922/1896) was sold by the BBÖ in 1927 to the GKB, where it operated until December 1962. Although a product of Wiener Neustadt, No 406 is seen in July 1961 running with a Floridsdorf-built boiler, which it has received at some time from a classmate. *Phil Tatt/Online Transport Archive*

Opposite below: No 674 (StEG 507/1860) awaits its next duty at Graz GKB shed in July 1961. The last four members of the veteran former Südbahn Class 29 remained in service with the GKB until the 1960s, achieving an impressive working life of more than 100 years. *Phil Tatt/Online Transport Archive*

Above: No 30.109 (StEG 2809/1900) leaves Leibnitz on 21 May 1964 with train No LW 51, the 7.55am departure to Wies-Eibiswald, where it was due to arrive at 10am. The elegant 2-6-2Ts of Class 30 were designed by Karl Gölsdorf for the Vienna *Stadtbahn*, and a total of 113 were built between 1895 and 1901. The GKB acquired 13 members of the class from the BBÖ between 1931 and 1936 – including No 30.109 in 1932 – which were used mainly on passenger services. All members of the class were withdrawn by the end of the 1960s. *Charles Firminger/Online Transport Archive*

Left: No 30.109 is seen at Muggenau-Silberberg on the Sulmtalbahn with train No LW 51, the 7.55am from Leibnitz to Wies-Eibiswald on 21 May 1964. Services on the Sulmtalbahn finished three years later, on 27 May 1967 for passengers, with the last freight loads moving four days later. *Charles Firminger/Online Transport Archive*

Above: On the same day, No 30.109 is engaged in shunting its mixed train at Heimschuh, 7.3km from Leibnitz. Following withdrawal, No 30.109 spent several years in the sidings at Graz together with other out of service locomotives, before subsequently being preserved. *Charles Firminger/Online Transport Archive*

Right: No 1851 (Krauss, Linz 3932/1898), seen at Köflach on 21 May 1964, was one of two locomotives of its type, built in 1898, which found their way in 1926 from the BBÖ to the GKB, where they were used mainly on shunting duties. No 1851 was taken out of traffic in 1966, and for many years it stood patiently in the sidings at Graz, awaiting eventual preservation. Sister locomotive No 1852 was sold in 1968 to the steelworks at Judenburg, where it would be withdrawn in 1975. *Charles Firminger/Online Transport Archive*

Opposite above: No 372 (Floridsdorf 768/1891) basks in the sun at the GKB shed at Graz on 21 May 1964. After withdrawal on 2 May 1968, No 372 was preserved by the Austrian Railway Museum. *Charles Firminger/Online Transport Archive*

Opposite below: In another view on 21 May 1964, No 674 (StEG 507/1860) stands next to the turntable at Graz. Acquired by the GKB in 1924, No 674 was withdrawn on 8 January 1965 at the impressive age of 105 years, and moved in 1968 to the Budapest Transport Museum. *Charles Firminger/Online Transport Archive*

Above: Class 56 (originally Class 170) was an 8-coupled two-cylinder compound freight locomotive, of which almost 800 examples were built from 1897 onwards for the kkStB and the Südbahn. No 56.3268 (Wiener Neustadt 5509/1919) departs Graz, GKB station on 21 May 1964 with train No 6735, the 5.14pm from Graz Hauptbahnhof to Wies-Eibiswald, where it is due to arrive at 7.15pm. Originally kkStB No 170.679, ÖBB No 56.3268 was acquired by the Graz-Köflacher Bahn in 1951, and finally withdrawn in 1970. *Charles Firminger/Online Transport Archive*

Right: A short time later on the evening of 21 May 1964, No 372 has left the GKB locomotive shed, and passes over the level crossing on its way to propel a rake of empty coaching stock to Graz Hauptbahnhof to form the 6.30pm departure to Köflach. *Charles Firminger/Online Transport Archive*

Below: At about 6pm on the evening of 21 May 1964, No 56.3147 (Breitfeld, Danek & Co 103/1917) is shunting at Graz. Between 1948 and 1955 the GKB acquired 16 members of Class 56. The former kkStB No 170.331 arrived at the GKB in 1949 as its third member of Class 56, and was not withdrawn until 1973. *Charles Firminger/Online Transport Archive*

9. Gleisdorf – Weiz (StmLB)

The 15km long line from Gleisdorf, located between Graz and Feldbach, to Weiz, opened in 1889. 22 years later its importance increased with the opening of the 760mm gauge Feistritztalbahn from Weiz to Birkfeld in December 1911. The Gleisdorf-Weiz local railway company was dissolved In June 1942, and the concession for the line was taken over by the state of Steiermark.

The line made use of a series of second-hand steam locomotives, notably a pair of 2-6-2Ts, Nos 130.03 and 130.04, originally built as Nos 43 and 44 of the Gürbetalbahn in Switzerland, which later became part of the Bern-Lötschberg-Simplon-Bahn. The electrification of the BLS Group after World War 1 rendered them redundant with the BLS, and together with four sister locomotives they were acquired by the Österreichische Bundesbahnen (BBÖ), which at the time were suffering from a serious motive power shortage, becoming BBÖ Nos 130.01-06. Their use with the BBÖ was, however, of relatively short duration, and by 1928 all six locomotives had been taken out of service.

In 1928, No 130.04 was purchased by the Steiermärkische Landesbahnen, followed in 1929 by No 130.03, and for many years they formed the backbone of operations between Gleisdorf and Weiz. With their typically Swiss appearance Nos 130.03 and 130.04 were a great rarity in Austria.

The line was dieselised in 1964/65 with the arrival at Weiz of diesel locomotives Nos DE 1 and DE 2, but for many years a steam back-up remained in place, in the form of the former No 93.1420, acquired from the ÖBB in 1966, which operated as StmLB No 93.

No 130.03 (SLM 1669/1905) was one of a pair of attractive 2-6-2Ts acquired from the BBÖ for use on the line from Gleisdorf to Weiz. After some 36 years in service at Weiz, No 130.03 was withdrawn in 1965 and subsequently scrapped. *Author's Collection*

10. Out of Service

For many years, lines of out of use steam locomotives, made redundant by the relentless advance of diesel and electric traction, could be found standing silently in sidings at ÖBB depots. Often these locomotives remained officially in ÖBB stock long after being taken out of service, and would not officially be withdrawn until months, or even years later.

Even after final withdrawal took place, low scrap metal prices and a shortage of personnel or of contractors interested in taking on the work, meant that there was sometimes a long delay until redundant locomotives were finally cut up. Few of these locomotives would ever return to steam; instead, they lingered, slowly rusting away until their destiny eventually caught up with them.

Polish State Railways (PKP) Class PT31 was a 2-8-2 express locomotive, of which 98 examples were built between 1932 and 1938, followed by a further 12 delivered in 1940 to the order of the Deutsche Reichsbahn. After World War 2, three of the 1940 series were inherited by the ÖBB, becoming Class 919. Initially they were used on the Westbahn, but from the summer 1952 timetable they were transferred to operate on the Südbahn between Wien and Gloggnitz, based at Wien Süd. Following electrification of the Semmeringbahn in 1959, they were stored out of use. The three members of Class 919 were officially withdrawn on 5 July 1961, after which all three were scrapped. On 8 May 1959, No 919.166 (Krenau 795/1940) stands at Wien Hütteldorf in the company of several similarly redundant 2-8-4 locomotives of Class 12.
Charles Firminger/Online Transport Archive

Above: ÖBB Class 892 consisted of two 0-8-0Ts, which were built in 1944 for the military railway authorities, which numbered them as 4901 and 4902. In 1950 they came to the ÖBB in an exchange of locomotives with the Hungarian Railways (MÁV), and were employed thereafter on shunting duties at Knittelfeld. Both locomotives were officially withdrawn on 3 December 1962. No 892.01 (Krenau 1046/1944) is seen out of use at Knittelfeld with its classmate. *Author's Collection*

Above: Although not officially withdrawn until 20 October 1972, No 93.1404 (StEG 4828/1928) was already in a very derelict state when it was photographed at Wien Ost in February 1972, and had clearly already been out of service for a significant period of time. *Author's Collection*

Steam on the Narrow Gauge

In the late 19th and early 20th centuries a large number of narrow gauge railways were built on the territory of the present day Austrian Republic, most of them for the purpose of connecting more remote locations. At the outset of the building of narrow gauge lines, the so-called 'Bosnian gauge' of 760mm was selected to become the norm for most subsequent Austrian narrow gauge lines.

With the exception of the Salzkammergut-Lokalbahn and Zillertalbahn, which both remained independent, most narrow gauge lines were either absorbed by the BBÖ, succeeded following World War 2 by the ÖBB, or became part of the Steiermärkische Landesbahnen. This had the advantage of facilitating the standardisation of locomotives and rolling stock, and the common gauge allowed these to be transferred between the different lines.

A central feature of the story of narrow gauge railways in Austria is the remarkable 'U' class 0-6-2T, developed from locomotives introduced in 1889 for the Steyrtalbahn, and in 1890 for the Salzkammergut-Lokalbahn, which became in effect the standard Austrian narrow gauge locomotive. The highly successful 'U' class was built in large quantities for different Austrian lines, and would later be developed in both compound and superheated versions. Members of the 'U' class (as ÖBB Class 298), together with the compound version, Class Uv (ÖBB Class 298.2), remained in service until the last years of ÖBB narrow gauge steam.

The introduction of diesel traction began as early as the 1930s, but whilst the early diesel locomotives demonstrated their usefulness, they were not powerful enough to replace steam completely. Although new steam classes were introduced in the 1920s, locomotives from the 1890s and early 1900s would remain indispensable on most narrow gauge lines as late as the 1950s and 1960s.

The years following World War 2 brought some relief for the ageing motive power fleets in the form of military (*Heeresfeldbahn*) locomotives, which found themselves in Austria at the end of the war, in particular several almost brand new members of Class KDL 11 (HF 160 D). The ÖBB put three of these into service as 0-8-0TT tender tanks (Class 699), as well as four more which it rebuilt as tank locomotives (Class 699.1). A further example found its way to the Salzkammergut-Lokalbahn, relocating subsequently to the Feistritztalbahn. Two 0-4-0T and 0-6-0T locomotives from Henschel became ÖBB Nos 698.01 and 898.01, and were used for shunting purposes. Four Class HF 110C 0-6-0TTs were employed by the ÖBB on secondary duties as Classes 798 and 798.1, but they were not very popular, and their working lives with the ÖBB were of short duration. Three further HF 110C locomotives were acquired by the StmLB, whilst the Salzkammergut-Lokalbahn also had two – although these were both withdrawn by 1955. A notable former *Heeresfeldbahn* locomotive was an impressive 0-10-0TT (Class HF 210 E), built by Borsig in 1939, which became Salzkammergut-Lokalbahn No 22, and later operated on the Zillertalbahn.

Delivery of the powerful Class 2095 B-B diesel-hydraulic locomotives between 1958 and 1962 transformed the nature of operations on the ÖBB narrow gauge lines. In particular, the arrival of members of Class 2095 finally displaced steam power from both the Ybbstalbahn and the Pinzgauer Lokalbahn. Of the ÖBB lines, only the Vellachtalbahn and the Steyrtalbahn remained entirely steam operated. Had just a few more members of Class 2095 been built, it is certain that steam operations would not have continued as long as they did on the Waldviertelbahn. The Steiermärkische Landesbahnen ordered their own large diesels, supplied by BBC/ÖAMG, six of which were put into service between 1965 and 1967, largely eliminating steam from the StmLB's narrow gauge lines.

Although all the significant narrow gauge lines survived until the late 1950s, this would not continue. The first victim was the much loved Salzkammergut-Lokalbahn, which closed in 1957. Although services on the other lines continued into the 1960s, both passenger and goods traffic declined steadily, due to the relentless growth of road traffic, and there was a general lack of investment in the ÖBB's narrow gauge lines. In 1971 the Vellachtalbahn, which had been without passenger services since 1965, was the first ÖBB narrow gauge line to be closed. A few months later the same fate befell the Gurktalbahn, where passenger services had ended in 1968. The Steyrtalbahn's short branch to Sierning closed on new year's day 1967, and from the following year passenger services were replaced by buses between Molln and Klaus, although freight services to Klaus continued.

The Steiermärkische Landesbahnen's lines were not spared. Passenger services on the Lokalbahn Kapfenberg–Au-Seewiesen (the 'Thörlerbahn') ended as early as 1958, and in 1964 the length of the line was reduced by 3km. On the Feistritztalbahn all traffic was withdrawn between Birkfeld and Ratten in 1971, and passenger services on the remainder of the line ended just two years later. In 1973 passenger services were also withdrawn from the last 11km of the Murtalbahn between Tamsweg and Mauterndorf.

Opposite: Salzkammergut-Lokalbahn 0-6-2T No 10 (Krauss, Linz 2822/1893) has arrived at St Wolfgang on 16 August 1956 with a train from Bad Ischl to Salzburg. The attractive metal numbers on the cab side were a characteristic feature of these locomotives.
John McCann/Online Transport Archive

1. The Salzkammergut-Lokalbahn

The Salzkammergut-Lokalbahn (SKGLB) is perhaps the most famous of Austria's narrow gauge railways, and thanks to its unique history, its fascinating motive power and rolling stock fleets, and the beautiful scenery through which it travelled, it has attained an almost mythical status in the years since its closure. The first 9.6km von Bad Ischl Lokalbahnhof to Strobl were opened in 1890. The following year a further, separate section was opened from Salzburg to Mondsee (35.9km), and in 1893 these two sections were linked by a connecting section between St Lorenz and Strobl via St Gilgen and St Wolfgang. The completed SKGLB consisted of the 63.2km 'main line' from Bad Ischl to Salzburg Lokalbahnhof, and a 3.5km-long branch line from St Lorenz to Mondsee.

Although the first section of the line was opened with a pair of small 0-4-0Ts built by Krauss, Linz in 1890, the 'standard' SKGLB locomotive was a class of 10 elegant 0-6-2Ts, based on the first Steyrtalbahn locomotives, which were built by Krauss, Linz between 1890 and 1906. They were predecessors of the later near-omnipresent 'U' class. One of the 0-4-0Ts and two of the 0-6-2Ts were requisitioned in 1918 by the military, and never returned, and locomotive No 6 was scrapped in 1948 following a derailment. In compensation, however, the motive power fleet received two additions in the 1920s, and a further two in 1942, and was supplemented following World War 2 by several former *Heeresfeldbahn* locomotives.

In spite of continuing high passenger traffic figures, proposals for electrification that were sadly never realised, and considerable local opposition against its closure, the 'Ischlerbahn' fell victim to a lack of political support and a desire to utilise parts of the trackbed for road improvements, and in 1957 it was the first significant line in Austria to be closed. To the great regret of many, the final scheduled SKGLB passenger train ran on 30 September 1957, and goods services ended on 10 October.

Right: No 7 (Krauss, Linz 2751/1892) has its supplies of coal and water replenished at St Lorenz, junction for the branch to Mondsee, on 16 August 1956. Three weeks later, on 5 September 1956, No 7 derailed and overturned as a result of a collision with a lorry on a level crossing at Kraiwiesen. Fortunately, the accident did not result in any major injuries, and No 7 was not seriously damaged. Following the closure of the SKGLB in October 1957, locomotives Nos 7, 11 and 12 were acquired by the Steiermärkische Landesbahnen, and put into service as Nos S7, S11 and S12. *John McCann/ Online Transport Archive*

Below: The last coaches in the train behind No 7 are typical SKGLB four-wheelers Nos 552 and 553, built in 1906 and 1893 respectively. *John McCann/Online Transport Archive*

Above: SKGLB No 11 (Krauss, Linz 3034/1894) pauses at St Wolfgang with a train from Salzburg to Bad Ischl on 16 August 1956. *John McCann/Online Transport Archive*

Right: Almost a year after the closure of the SKGLB, a number of items of rolling stock still stood out of use at Salzburg Itzling works on 7 September 1958. Amongst them was 0-6-0T No 30 (Orenstein & Koppel 13573/1940), which together with sister locomotive No 31 was formerly employed primarily on the short branch line from St Lorenz to Mondsee, and on shunting duties at Salzburg.
John McCann/Online Transport Archive

2. The Steyrtalbahn (ÖBB)

As the first 760mm narrow gauge line in Austria, the Steyrtalbahn was the predecessor of many subsequent lines. It was built in stages, initially in 1889 from Garsten, where it met the standard gauge line between St Valentin and Kleinreifling, to Grünburg (19.2km), and the following year to Agonitz (31.7km). Finally, in 1909 the line was extended to Klaus (39.8km), where it connected with the Pyhrnbahn from Linz to Selzthal. In 1891 a branch was opened from Pergern to Bad Hall (15.4km), but the section between Sierning and Bad Hall was closed in 1933, and later dismantled. Services on the remaining 4.8km section

of the branch, between Pergern and Sierning, continued to operate until 1 January 1967.

Following World War 2 there was a failure to invest in improvements and strengthening of the track, which meant that the new Class 2095 narrow gauge diesel locomotives could not be used, and the Steyrtalbahn remained entirely steam operated.

In 1968 passenger services between Molln and Klaus were replaced by buses, but for the time being goods services continued to operate over the entire length of the line, with large quantities of timber being transferred onto the standard gauge in the exchange sidings at Klaus.

From Garsten to Klaus with No 298.106 in May 1959

Opposite below: On Sunday
10 May 1959, No 298.106 (Krauss,
Linz 6925/1914) waits with a train
of empty stock at Garsten depot
before moving into the station and
commencing its journey to Klaus.
In 1914, the Steyrtalbahn ordered
a sixth locomotive from Krauss,
Linz – No 6 *Klaus*, which
represented a slightly modified
version of the original Steyrtalbahn
locomotives. No 6 differed from its
five predecessors particularly
through its shorter smokebox and
longer side tanks, as well as the
coal bunker being relocated to the
back of the cab. *Charles Firminger/
Online Transport Archive*

Above right: With its lengthy
train consisting of a mixture of
traditional four-wheel coaches,
No 298.106 pauses at the
intermediate station at Molln.
Five years later in August 1964
No 298.106 would be sent to
the locomotive dump at
Obergrafendorf, although its
official withdrawal did not take
effect until 22 November 1972.
*Charles Firminger/Online Transport
Archive*

Right: No 298.106 has reached
the attractive terminus station at
Klaus. To the left are the standard
gauge tracks of the Pyhrnbahn.
There was just a single narrow
gauge line in front of the station
building, so the locomotive had to
push the train back in order to run
round. *Charles Firminger/
Online Transport Archive*

A visit to the Steyrtalbahn in April 1966

Left: On Saturday 9 April 1966, No 298.56 (Floridsdorf 1354/1900) leaves Garsten with train No GK 23, the 7.50am from Garsten to Klaus, due to arrive at Klaus at 9.58am. *Charles Firminger/Online Transport Archive*

Below: No 298.52 (Krauss, Linz 3710/1898) passes Sarning with a goods train from Garsten (departing at 8.20am) to Klaus on Saturday 9 April 1966. *Charles Firminger/Online Transport Archive*

Above: On 9 April 1966, No 298.102 (Krauss, Linz 1994/1889) stands at Pergern with train No PS 53, the 1.02pm from Garsten to Sierning, due to depart Pergern at 1.32pm. One of the first three Steyrtalbahn locomotives, No 298.102 was delivered in 1889 as No 2 *Sierning*. Although officially withdrawn on 15 March 1973, like No 298.106 it had already arrived at Obergrafendorf dump by the late 1960s. *Charles Firminger/Online Transport Archive*

Right: No 298.102 has reached its destination at Sierning, where it was due at 1.51pm. The service will return as train No PS 52, the 2.22pm from Sierning to Garsten. At the time this train, which ran Monday-Saturday, was the only service on Saturdays between Garsten and Sierning. From Monday to Friday there was a second working, departing Sierning at 5.50am, with the return service leaving Garsten at 5.52pm. *Charles Firminger/Online Transport Archive*

Left: No 298.14 (Krauss, Linz 3816/1898) stands at rest outside the two-road shed at Garsten on 10 May 1959. 11 years later, No 298.14 was withdrawn on 5 June 1970 and sold to the society Eurovapor, which would operate No 298.14 on tourist services on the Waldenburgerbahn in Switzerland. *Charles Firminger/Online Transport Archive*

Below: From left to right, Nos 298.51 (Krauss, Linz 3709/1898), 298.27 (StEG 3062/1903) and 298.56 (Floridsdorf 1354/1900) await their next duties at Garsten shed in the early morning of 9 April 1966. Although No 298.27 was withdrawn on 25 October 1973 and later scrapped, its two older classmates would continue in operation on the Steyrtalbahn until the end of services. *Charles Firminger/ Online Transport Archive*

Above: No 298.52 is seen near Pergern on 9 April 1966 with train GK 18, the 2.32pm from Klaus to Garsten, due to arrive at Garsten at 4.28pm. *Charles Firminger/Online Transport Archive*

Right: No 498.04 (Krauss, Linz 1512/1929) stands out of service at Garsten on 9 April 1966, dreaming of better days. Three members of Class 498 operated on the Steyrtalbahn, Nos 498.04, 498.07 and 498.08, which had been displaced from Waidhofen and Zell am See by dieselisation. The use of Class 498, which operated notably on heavy limestone trains between Molln and Klaus, lasted only from 1963 to 1967. *Charles Firminger/ Online Transport Archive*

Opposite above: On 21 August 1967, No 298.56 approaches Klaus, where it is due to arrive at 9.58am, with train No GK 23, the 7.50am from Garsten. *Author's Collection*

Opposite below: No 298.51 (Krauss, Linz 3709/1898) stands at Grünburg with a train for Molln in the summer of 1969. *Author's Collection*

Above: Around January 1973, No 298.56 stands with a rake of empty coaching stock at Garsten depot, waiting to form the next departure. *Charles Whetmath*

A goods train with No 699.103

Below: No 699.103 (Franco Belge 2821/1944) brings a rather modest goods train along the Steyr valley, circa January 1973. *Charles Whetmath*

Opposite above: No 699.103 has arrived at Grünburg, where it will collect further wagons, and add them to the train before continuing its journey. *Charles Whetmath*

Opposite below: Having added three goods vans to its train, No 699.103 departs from Grünburg station, running between the river and the impressive background of the town of Grünburg. *Charles Whetmath*

3. The Ybbstalbahn (ÖBB)

The Ybbstalbahn was a lengthy 760mm gauge line which had its operational centre and principal depot at Waidhofen an der Ybbs, on the standard gauge line from Amstetten to Kleinreifling and Hieflau. The first section, from Waidhofen to Groß Hollenstein (25.5km), which followed the wandering course of the Ybbs, opened in 1896, and in 1898 the line was extended to Lunz am See (53.5km). Lunz was the starting point of the spectacular and steeply graded last 17.4km to Kienberg-Gaming (70.9km), opened later in 1898, where the narrow gauge line connected with the standard gauge branch from Pöchlarn. In 1899 a 5.7km branch was opened from Gstadt (5.4km from Waidhofen) to Ybbsitz.

Although various narrow gauge classes operated on the Ybbstalbahn, in particular members of the famous 'U' class (ÖBB Class 298) and later developments of the design as ÖBB Classes 298.2, 398 and 498, for many years the Ybbstalbahn was home to Class Yv, three compound 0-6-4Ts built in 1896, which were specially developed for the line. Class Yv was notable as the only narrow gauge type to be designed by Karl Gölsdorf, Chief Engineer of the *kaiserlich-königliche Staatsbahnen* (kkStB). Problems with the operation of the trailing bogie led to frequent derailments when running in reverse, and although the issue was resolved by a fitting the three 'Yvs' with a revised bogie design, the choice for further orders went in favour of the dependable and cheaper 'U' class, and no further members of Class Yv (which would later become ÖBB Class 598) were built.

An interesting feature of the last years of steam operations was the presence of the former *Heeresfeldbahn* 0-4-0T No 698.01, which found employment on station pilot duties at Waidhofen. With the advance of dieselisation, especially the arrival of four members of Class 2095 from 1962, the use of members of Class 598 on the Ybbstalbahn ended the same year, with Nos 598.02 and 598.03 both being transferred to Gmünd. The following year, No 398.01 as well as all three members of Class 298.2 also left Waidhofen. The final steam duties on the Ybbstalbahn were performed by No 498.07, until finally it too departed on 3 July 1966.

No 298.205 (Krauss, Linz 4785/1902) stands with its train at Kienberg-Gaming on 9 May 1959. To the right is the terminus of the standard gauge line to Pöchlarn. A member of Class 770 quenches its thirst beside the locomotive shed. *Charles Firminger/Online Transport Archive*

A journey on the Ybbstalbahn in May 1959

Left: Since leaving Kienberg-Gaming (elevation 391m), No 298.205 has overcome gradients of up to 3.1% (1 in 32), to reach the summit of the line at Pfaffenschlag (694m) after 11km. From the attractively located station at Pfaffenschlag the line descends towards Lunz am See. *Charles Firminger/Online Transport Archive*

Below: No 298.205 awaits departure from Pfaffenschlag. At the end of World War 2, the former DRB No 98 801 found itself with the Czechoslovak Railways (ČSD), which renumbered it as U37.101. At the end of 1950, however, it was reunited with its two classmates in Austria. The ÖBB numbered them as Nos 298.205-207. No 298.205 operated on the Ybbstalbahn until 1962, but by 1963 it was standing in the narrow gauge locomotive dump at Obergrafendorf. It was officially withdrawn on 29 June 1973. *Charles Firminger/Online Transport Archive*

Left: No 298.205 has arrived at Lunz am See, where it is replaced by No 498.07 (Floridsdorf 3037/1931) for the journey onwards to Waidhofen. The members of Class 498 were built between 1928 and 1931 as the final development of Austrian narrow gauge steam design, but they were all withdrawn by 1973. *Charles Firminger/ Online Transport Archive*

Below: No 298.205 stands at Lunz am See. In 1902 and 1905 the Niederösterreichische Landesbahnen (NÖLB) ordered three powerful compound 0-6-2T locomotives of Class Uv, which were based on the successful 'U' class and were intended for use on the Waldviertelbahn system in Niederösterreich and the lower sections of the Mariazellerbahn. As ÖBB Nos 298.205-207, all three locomotives operated on the Ybbstalbahn during the 1950s and early 1960s, based at Waidhofen shed. *Author's Collection*

Opposite above: Nos 498.07 and 298.205 stand side by side at Lunz. Class 298.2, originally Class Uv, was a non-superheated compound locomotive fitted with Walschaerts valve gear. By contrast, Class 498, built between 1928 and 1931 as Class Uh, was a superheated locomotive, with the significantly larger boiler compared with the 'U' class having to be placed higher because of the decision to abandon the use of outside frames under the cab. The first examples were fitted with Caprotti valve gear, but this was not a great success, and the two 1931-built examples instead had Lentz poppet valves. *Author's Collection*

Opposite below: Who would not want to be on board, as No 498.07 makes its leisurely way along the beautiful valley of the Ybbs on a sunny day in May 1959? Seven years later, No 498.07 would be the last steam locomotive to leave the Ybbstalbahn, departing in July 1966. *Charles Firminger/ Online Transport Archive*

No 598.03 (Krauss, Linz 3358/1896) pauses at Groß Hollenstein with a passenger train. Three members of Class Yv were built for the opening of the first section of the Ybbstalbahn in 1896. As ÖBB Class 598, they continued to earn their keep in their Ybbs valley home territory until the 1960s, but the arrival of the powerful Class 2095 diesels at the start of the 1960s rendered them redundant. No 598.03 spent nearly its entire life on its home line, but in April 1962 it was transferred, together with sister locomotive No 598.02, to the Waldviertelbahn at Gmünd. However, after just a few months of use at Gmünd it was taken out of service, and finally sent to Obergrafendorf. *Author's Collection*

4. The Vellachtalbahn (ÖBB)

The Vellachtalbahn in Kärnten (Carinthia) in the south of Austria, opened in October 1902, ran 17.5km from Völkermarkt-Kühnsdorf, on the standard gauge line between Klagenfurt and Bleiburg, to Eisenkappel. Although passenger figures were relatively modest, the line carried considerable goods traffic – in particular to and from the pulp mill at Rechberg (14.1km) and a sawmill at Eisenkappel.

To address the requirement for a more powerful locomotive, in 1924 Krauss, Linz delivered the first of a new class. No Kh1 was an impressive 0-10-0T with the first four axles mounted in inside frames, and the fifth as a Klien-Lindner axle in outside frames at the rear of the locomotive. No Kh1, later ÖBB No 499.01, was fitted with a Giesl ejector in 1956, and spent its working life on the Vellachtalbahn until in 1963 it followed the path of so many ÖBB narrow gauge locomotives to the dump at Obergrafendorf. Various locomotives operated on the line during the years after World War 2, especially former *Heeresfeldbahn* Class KDL 11 locomotives of Classes 699.0 (0-8-0TT) and 699.1 (0-8-0T), as well as 0-8-2Ts Nos 199.02 and 199.03. Motive power shortages, resulting from locomotives being taken out of service when overhauls fell due, led to Engerths Nos 399.01 and 399.03 spending periods on loan in 1969 and 1971.

In the years following World War 2 there was a sharp decline in passenger traffic, and a relatively minor derailment in January 1965 was used as a pretext to withdraw passenger services with immediate effect. Goods services were suspended on the last 3.4km between Rechberg and Eisenkappel on 2 May 1965, and two years later the rails on this section were removed.

The pulp mill at Rechberg continued to generate large volumes of freight – especially chlorine gas, which for safety reasons was not permitted to be transported by road. By 1971 improvements to the local roads enabled loads for the pulp mill to be transferred from rail to road transport, and the Vellachtalbahn was the first ÖBB narrow gauge line to be completely closed and dismantled. On 22 May 1971, the final goods train, consisting of a guard's van and four standard gauge wagons on transporter wagons, was brought from Rechberg to Völkermarkt-Kühnsdorf by No 699.103.

No 699.01, formerly *Heeresfeldbahn* No HF 2818, waits at Eisenkappel before starting the return journey to Völkermarkt-Kühnsdorf on 6 September 1963. All passenger services on the Vellachtalbahn were withdrawn 16 months later in January 1965. *Author's Collection*

Opposite above: With combined forces Nos 699.103 (Franco Belge 2821/1944) and 699.01 (Franco Belge 2818/1944) have brought their train to Völkermarkt-Kühnsdorf on 6 September 1963. They represent the two ÖBB variants of the former *Heeresfeldbahn* Class KDL 11 (also known as Class HF 160D) – one rebuilt as a simple tank locomotive and the other as a tender-tank, as built. *Author's Collection*

Opposite below: The well cared-for No 699.01 waits for its next duty at Völkermarkt-Kühnsdorf in 1965. Its last day in service was 20 September 1967, after which it was set aside on the expiry of its boiler certificate. *Author's Collection*

Above: The end draws near. No 699.103 is engaged in shunting at Völkermarkt-Kühnsdorf in the final days of operations. On 22 May 1971 No 699.103 hauled the last goods train on the Vellachtalbahn. After operating the demolition trains it was transferred to Garsten for use on the Steyrtalbahn. *Author's Collection*

5. The Gurktalbahn (ÖBB)

The 760mm gauge Gurktalbahn, opened in October 1898, connected at Treibach-Althofen with the Klagenfurt – Leoben main line, and ran a distance of 28.8km to Klein Glödnitz.

The locomotive fleet consisted originally of three small 0-6-2T locomotives of kkStB Class T, the design of which was derived largely from that of the 'U' class, but which were much less powerful than their larger cousins. Despite this, they enjoyed great popularity on the gently graded Gurktalbahn. All three members of Class T which were based at Treibach survived to become ÖBB Class 198 following World War 2, but the three members of Class 198 were withdrawn by 1960. Attempts by enthusiasts to save No 198.01 for preservation were unsuccessful, and sadly it was scrapped.

In ÖBB days services were operated by members of the near-universal Class 298, as well as 0-8-2Ts Nos 199.02 and 199.03,

originally built as Niederösterreichische Landesbahnen Class P, together with pre-war diesel locomotives of Class 2091.

As was the case for so many narrow gauge lines, passenger figures on the Gurktalbahn declined steadily in the 1950s and 1960s, which resulted in all passenger services being withdrawn in November 1968. The remaining freight services continued only as far as Gurk (17km), and the line was dismantled beyond Gurk. Goods trains continued to operate as required between Treibach and Gurk, until complete closure took place in February 1972. The tracks were removed, with the exception of a short section of approximately 3km between Treibach-Althofen and Pöckstein-Zwischenwässern, which opened as Austria's first preserved railway in 1974.

Opposite: No 298.54 (Krauss, Linz 3870/1898) waits at Treibach-Althofen on 7 May 1959 with a train for Klein Glödnitz. No 298.54 first came to the Gurktalbahn in the 1930s, and was subsequently transferred on several occasions between Treibach-Althofen and Völkermarkt-Kühnsdorf, before in November 1951 it made its way one last time to Treibach-Althofen, which would be its last depot. *Author's Collection*

Above and right: The train pauses at the well-kept station at Straßburg, 12.6km from Treibach-Althofen. No 298.54 was already stored out of service at Treibach-Althofen in November 1960, and made its way in July 1963 to the locomotive dump at Obergrafendorf. Despite this, it would not be formally withdrawn until November 1972. *Charles Firminger/Online Transport Archive*

Opposite above: On 5 September 1959, a Railway Correspondence and Travel Society (RCTS) tour of Austria visited the Gurktalbahn. 0-8-2T No 199.02 (Krauss, Linz 1467/1926) waits with the RCTS special train at Treibach-Althofen station. *Author's Collection*

Opposite below: No 199.02 has reached the terminus at Klein Glödnitz with the special train. No 199.02 first came to the Gurktalbahn in July 1958, but stayed for only three months before being transferred to the Waldviertelbahn at Gmünd. However, as soon as May 1959 it returned to Treibach-Althofen, where it would stay for more than nine years, before moving to the Vellachtalbahn at Völkermarkt-Kühnsdorf in 1968. *Author's Collection*

Above: No 199.03 (Krauss, Linz 1468/1926) stands out of use at Treibach-Althofen beneath the timber-built extension at the side of the locomotive shed. No 199.03 first came to the Gurktalbahn from Gmünd in April 1960, but was transferred away to Zell am See in October of the same year. Just three weeks later, however, it was transferred back to Treibach-Althofen, where it was allocated until July 1968, when it moved, with classmate No 199.02, to its last shed at Völkermarkt-Kühnsdorf on the Vellachtalbahn. *Author's Collection*

6. The Waldviertelbahn (ÖBB)

The Waldviertelbahn system, with its centre at Gmünd in Niederösterreich, next to the Czech border, on the Vienna-Prague main line, consisted of two distinct elements. The northern line, from Gmünd via Alt Nagelberg (11.4km) to Litschau (25.4km), with a 13.2km branch from Alt Nagelberg to Heidenreichstein, opened in 1900. The southern line from Gmünd via Weitra (14km) opened in 1902 as far as Steinbach-Groß Pertholz (24.1km). A noteworthy feature of the section between Alt Weitra and Weitra was a large reverse loop, which enabled the line to gain height in order to climb above the plain which it had traversed from Gmünd. Even with this loop, trains still had to work hard to overcome a difference in elevation of no less than 68 metres over a distance of 4.2km, representing an average gradient of 1.6% (1 in 62). In 1903 the southern line was extended over the steeply graded and highly scenic section beyond Steinbach-Groß Pertholz through the hills to the terminus at Groß Gerungs (43km).

The narrow gauge lines of the Waldviertel region were initially operated by members of the near-omnipresent 'U' class. Various other locomotive types featured over the years, including Class Uv, built between 1902 and 1905 as an enlarged, compound version of the highly successful 'U' class.

In later years, the Waldviertel narrow gauge lines became well known as the last preserve of Class 399, a powerful, superheated Engerth design, which was delivered to the Niederösterreichische Landesbahnen (NÖLB) by Krauss, Linz in 1906 and 1908 as Class Mh for use on the Mariazellerbahn. From the 1970s, all six members of Class 399 were based at Gmünd, together with No 298.207, the last operational example of Class Uv. Despite the presence of diesel traction, the six remarkable Class 399 Engerths and No 298.207 continued to prove their value, working for many years side-by-side with the diesels.

Class 399 Engerth No 399.06 (Krauss, Linz 5925/1908) has overcome the challenging climb from Alt Weitra, and arrived at the attractive station at Weitra with its goods train for Groß Gerungs in July 1971. Of interest are the two brake wagons, being used in conjunction with bolster wagons which are not equipped with through braking. *Author's Collection*

No 399.04 (Krauss, Linz 5434/1906) waits with a mixed train for Litschau at the narrow gauge platform at Gmünd in 1969. The narrow gauge station at Gmünd lay directly beside the road, opposite the standard gauge station. *Author's Collection*

No 298.207 (Krauss, Linz 5329/1905), originally delivered as NÖLB No 22, later No Uv.3, stands in the long siding at the narrow gauge depot at Gmünd in 1969. Until the end of steam traction on the Waldviertelbahn this siding often contained up to three locomotives, either available for use or sometimes set aside in need of repairs. Long after sister locomotives Nos 298.205 and 298.206 had been taken out of service, No 298.207 continued in use on the Waldviertelbahn as the last member of its class in service with the ÖBB. *Author's Collection*

Left: No 598.03 (Krauss, Linz 3358/1896), which for many years had operated on its home system, the Ybbstalbahn, came to the Waldviertelbahn at the end of its working life. It spent two years at Gmünd between May 1962 and June 1964, but was only actually in service for a few months. Its working days at an end, No 598.03 is seen in store at Gmünd depot in 1963. *Author's Collection*

Below: Freshly repainted No 399.01 (Krauss, Linz 5431/1906), originally delivered as NÖLB No 50, later No Mh.1, stands with a freight train at the well-kept station at Weitra, on the southern line of the Waldviertelbahn system, between Gmünd and Groß Gerungs. *Author's Collection*

Above: No 399.05 (Krauss, Linz 5924/1908) leaves Alt Nagelberg with train No GN 53, the 1.22pm mixed service from Gmünd to Heidenreichstein on 11 June 1971. The lines to Litschau and Heidenreichstein divided at Alt Nagelberg, but initially ran beside one another, which led to the famous parallel departures from Alt Nagelberg. The rails on the right-hand side of this view are the line to Litschau. *Author's Collection*

Right: Also on 11 June 1971, No 298.207 leaves the halt at Schönau, not very far from the terminus at Litschau, with its short mixed train. No 298.207 was the last compound steam locomotive operated by the ÖBB. *Author's Collection*

Above: Trains from Gmünd to Groß Gerungs would stop at Steinbach-Groß Pertholz (24.1km from Gmünd) to take water before they did battle with the especially twisting and steeply graded section of line from Steinbach to Langschlag. On 8 April 1972 it is the turn of No 399.02 (Krauss, Linz 5432/1906). The lovely scenery of the Waldviertel region is apparent in this view. *Chris Gammell*

Opposite: Engerth No 399.02 waits to depart from Steinbach-Groß Pertholz on 8 April 1972 with a goods train from Gmünd to Groß Gerungs. The section of line which lies ahead crosses the central European watershed between the tributaries of the North Sea and the Black Sea. *Chris Gammell*

7. The Pinzgauer Lokalbahn (ÖBB)

The Pinzgauer Lokalbahn from Zell am See, situated on the main line between Schwarzach-St Veit and Wörgl, to Krimml (52.7km), opened in January 1898. The locomotive and rolling stock depot was located at Tischlerhäusl, 1.5km from the station at Zell am See. Plans for an extension, which would have created a connection with the Zillertalbahn, were never realised.

Following their introduction at Zell am See after World War 1, members of the 'U' class (later ÖBB Class 298) formed the backbone of services on the Pinzgauer Lokalbahn for many years, assisted by the superheated locomotives of Class Uh (ÖBB Class 498) following their introduction in 1928-29. After World War 2 the motive power fleet was reinforced by the arrival of former *Heeresfeldbahn* locomotives, in particular two members of *Heeresfeldbahn* Class KDL 11 (ÖBB Class 699). An interesting one-off locomotive which spent 20 years on the line was the sole member of Class 998, which was also inherited from the *Heeresfeldbahn* after the war.

Diesel traction arrived on the line in the 1930s in the form of BBÖ Class 2041/s (ÖBB Class 2091), followed in the 1950s by Class 2092

for shunting duties at Zell am See, but it was only with the introduction of the high-performance Class 2095 diesel-hydraulics in the early 1960s that steam traction could be finally replaced. Steam workings on the Pinzgauer Lokalbahn ended in 1963 with the arrival of a fourth member of Class 2095.

No 298.25 (StEG 2998/1902) stands ready to depart from Krimml on 15 August 1956. Originally delivered to the Bregenzerwaldbahn between Bregenz and Bezau in 1902, it operated there until 1936, but then ran on the Pinzgauer Lokalbahn between 1936 and 1954, and returned there from 1955 until 1962. *John McCann/ Online Transport Archive*

Left: No 298.56 (Floridsdorf 1354/1900) has arrived at Zell am See with a train from Krimml on 17 August 1956. The first coach of the train belongs to a type known as 'Pinzgau coaches', built between 1937 and 1940 to modernise the coaching stock fleet. These are easily recognisable because of their streamlined body shape with distinctive curved ends. *John McCann/Online Transport Archive*

Below: Regular members of the locomotive fleet for many years, Nos 298.05 (Krauss, Linz 3804/1898) and 298.51 (Krauss, Linz 3709/1898) stand outside the shed at Tischlerhäusl. *Author's Collection*

Opposite above: No 298.51 (Krauss, Linz 3709/1898) stands at Zell am See depot on 12 September 1958. Built for the Niederösterreichische Landesbahnen (NÖLB), it was originally NÖLB No 5 (renumbered as U.1 from 1909, and later becoming BBÖ No 298.51), and operated on the Pielachtalbahn from St Pölten to Kirchberg an der Pielach. No 298.51 operated on the Pinzgauer Lokalbahn from the 1920s until April 1961, when it was transferred to the Steyrtalbahn.
John McCann/Online Transport Archive

Opposite below: No 998.01 (Krauss, München 7651/1920) was a 0-6-2T which was similar in design to the Austrian 'U' class. It was built for the Kreuznacher Kleinbahnen in the Hunsrück region of Germany, where it operated until the line's closure in 1936. In World War 2 the German *Heeresfeldbahn* brought it to the present day Austria, where it remained at the Pinzgauer Lokalbahn after 1945. Taken out of service in the 1960s, it was moved to the locomotive dump at Obergrafendorf (see page 129). On 12 September 1958, No 998.01 stands at its home depot at Tischlerhäusl.
John McCann/Online Transport Archive

Above: No 699.03 stands in steam at Tischlerhäusl in July 1961. Then numbered HF 2856, it was in service on the Pinzgauer Lokalbahn by 1946, together with sister locomotive No HF 2857. Although No HF 2857 was out of use after just two years, and subsequently left the line, No HF 2856, renumbered by the ÖBB as 699.03, was based at Zell am See until 1964, although stored unserviceable from 25 April 1962 following the expiry of its boiler certificate.
Phil Tatt/Online Transport Archive

8. Former Military Locomotives at Tischlerhäusl

By the start of World War 2, a military test centre had been established at Mittersill on the Pinzgauer Lokalbahn. By the end of the war a large quantity of narrow gauge rolling stock was stored in the Oberpinzgau region, partly located at the Mittersill test centre, but also distributed amongst stations along the line. In 1945 the locomotives and stock were relocated to Tischlerhäusl. In the post-war period they were gradually either disposed of to the ÖBB, which had first rights to them, or sold to third parties. Especially worthy of mention are three members of Heeresfeldbahn Class KDL 11 – Nos HF 2855, 2856 and 2857 – all built by Franco Belge in 1944. No HF 2855 would have a particularly interesting life. Initially it moved in 1946 to the Salzkammergut-Lokalbahn, from where it was sold in 1950 to the Steiermärkische Landesbahnen, which put it to work on the Feistritztalbahn between Weiz and Ratten. Nos 2856 and 2857 became ÖBB Nos 699.03 and 699.104, respectively.

If no buyer was found, the remaining locomotives were scrapped, but in 1956 a fascinating selection of narrow gauge steam and diesel locomotives could be found at Tischlerhäusl; including the five steam locomotives illustrated here.

No HF 116 (Henschel 6339/1904) was a 600mm gauge 0-6-0T field railway locomotive, known as an *Illing* – half of a *Zwilling* ('twin') pair, designed to operate back-to-back. It was part of an order for 24 such locomotives delivered to the Munich railway battalion. A total of 182 *Zwilling* units had been delivered by the start of World War 1. *John McCann/Online Transport Archive*

Above: No HF 27 (Krauss München 6942/1914), delivered to the Munich railway battalion in October 1914, was a 600mm gauge 0-8-0T *Brigadelok*; a type which was built in vast quantities for use in World War 1. The development of the much more powerful, eight-coupled *Brigadelok* led to an end to demand for *Zwilling* locomotives like No HF 116. *John McCann/ Online Transport Archive*

Right: Industrial 0-4-0T No HF 8 752 (Henschel 22494/1934) was originally delivered to Wahler & Co of Munich together with its sister locomotive, Henschel works No 22493. *John McCann/Online Transport Archive*

Above: No HF 6 751 (Henschel 19936/1923), was another industrial 0-4-0T, originally delivered to the firm Eisenindustrie zu Menden und Schwerte AG in Nordrhein-Westfalen. Behind it stands a further 0-4-0T – No HF 9 753 (O&K 7927/1918), which was built for the Rheinische Kalksandsteinwerke.
John McCann/Online Transport Archive

Left: A head-on view of No HF 6 751 (Henschel 19936/1923). All five locomotives illustrated here were officially transferred to the Austrian Control Bank on 20 January 1956. Seven months later they were still at Tischlerhäusl, where they were photographed on 15 August 1956.
John McCann/Online Transport Archive

Opposite: On 18 May 1964, No 999.02 (Krauss, Linz 3401/1897) departs Puchberg, and sets off for the summit at Hochschneeberg. *Charles Firminger/ Online Transport Archive*

9. The Schneebergbahn (ÖBB)

The metre gauge rack railway to the summit of the Schneeberg mountain in Niederösterreich was opened in September 1897. The Schneebergbahn utilised the Abt rack system, as had the Schafbergbahn, which commenced services four years earlier.

The line began at Puchberg am Schneeberg, where it connected with the standard gauge Südbahn branch from Wiener Neustadt. The line led to the summit station at Hochschneeberg (9.6km), the highest railway station in Austria, in the course of which it gained 1,218 metres in height, with a maximum gradient of almost 20% (1 in 5).

The line was operated by a fleet of five rack locomotives, built by Krauss, Linz in 1897/98 (Nos Z 1-Z 4) and 1900 (No Z 5). Under the

ÖBB they became Nos 999.01-05. The most significant and visible modification made to them was when they were equipped with Giesl ejectors in the 1950s. In 1974 the very similar No 999.101 was transferred from the Schafbergbahn to provide support for the hard-pressed members of Class 999.

Both the Schneebergbahn and Schafbergbahn were built as pure rack railways, with the locomotives driven solely by the pinion engaging with the rack rail. The locomotives' conventional wheels simply revolved loose on the axles, which mean that all lines, including sidings and within the locomotive shed, were equipped with rack rails.

Right: The first ÖBB narrow gauge rack locomotive to be fitted with a Giesl ejector was No 99 7303 (later renumbered as 999.03), which received an experimental version in October 1952. An improved design was fitted in October 1953, which delivered the desired improved performance and reduced coal consumption, together with reduced spark generation. As a result it was decided to fit Giesl ejectors to all Schneeberg and Schafberg locomotives. No 999.03, standing outside the shed at Puchberg, still carries a number plate with its former BBÖ number Zz3. *Author's Collection*

Opposite above: No 999.03 (Krauss, Linz 3402/1897) stands with its train at Puchberg am Schneeberg station on 18 May 1964. *Charles Firminger/Online Transport Archive*

Opposite below: No 999.02 brings its well-filled train back down towards Puchberg on a fine autumn day in September 1962. *Marc Dahlström*

Above: The crew of No 999.04 (Krauss, Linz 3750/1898) takes advantage of the opportunity to enjoy the tremendous view from the Schneeberg on 11 September 1964. *Author's Collection*

10. The Schafbergbahn (ÖBB)

Opened in August 1893 by the Salzkammergut-Localbahn-Aktiengesellschaft (SKGLB), the metre gauge Schafbergbahn, a rack railway operated on the Abt system, was built to exploit the developing tourist traffic in the Salzkammergut region to the east of Salzburg, an area famous for its lakes and mountains.

The line runs from St Wolfgang Schafbergbahnhof, where the depot is located, to the summit at Schafbergspitze station (5.9km), adjacent to the hotel of the same name. After departing St Wolfgang station the line proceeds through the residential area of St Wolfgang, with a maximum gradient of 6% (1 in 17), but this is followed by the main climb, with a relatively constant gradient to the summit. The line gains a total of 1,190 metres in height, with a maximum gradient of 25.5% (1 in 3.9). As is also the case on the Schneebergbahn, the locomotives are propelled entirely via the pinion drive, meaning that even those tracks which are located on level ground need to be equipped with rack rails.

For 70 years the line was operated exclusively by the six rack locomotives built by Krauss, Linz for its opening. Originally Nos Z 1-Z 6 of the SKGLB, after several changes of identity under different operators, in the 1950s they became ÖBB Nos 999.101-106. Following successful trials on the Schneebergbahn in 1953, all locomotives were fitted with Giesl ejectors by 1955. In 1964 two smart diesel-hydraulic railcars were delivered by Simmering-Graz-Pauker, and in 1974 No 999.106 was transferred to the Schneebergbahn, but Nos 999.102-106 continued in use at St Wolfgang.

Producing a volcanic exhaust, No 999.102 (Krauss, Linz 2745/1893) storms out of St Wolfgang on 16 August 1956, and begins its journey to the summit at Schafbergspitze. The train is still on the relatively easily graded section of line at St Wolfgang. *John McCann/Online Transport Archive*

Left: In August 1960, No 999.103 (Krauss, Linz 2746/1893), which was originally Schafbergbahn No Z 3, has arrived at Schafbergspitze station. *Phil Tatt/Online Transport Archive*

Below: No 999.104 (Krauss, Linz 2823/1893) arrives at Schafbergalpe with a descending train on 23 August 1967. *Author's Collection*

11. Obergrafendorf (ÖBB)

Obergrafendorf was a 760mm gauge junction station to the south of St Pölten, where the line to Wieselburg and Gresten diverged from the Mariazellerbahn line to Mariazell and Gußwerk. With the expansion of diesel traction on the ÖBB's narrow gauge lines, and the progressive reduction of operations on narrow gauge routes, Obergrafendorf became a remarkable location, where out of service steam locomotives of nearly every class were gathered together to stand in rows awaiting possible further use, or final withdrawal and scrapping.

The first locomotive to be sent for storage at Obergrafendorf was No 798.101 (Henschel 25982/1941), a former member of *Heeresfeldbahn* Class HF 110 C, which arrived in July 1958 and would remain for 14 years. In the 1960s a large number and variety of locomotives could be found in the sidings at Obergrafendorf, exposed to the elements all year round, and slowly rusting away. In many cases these locomotives would not officially be withdrawn until several years after they first arrived at Obergrafendorf, and they had often reached an advanced state of dereliction by the time they were formally removed from ÖBB stock.

A visit to the sidings at Obergrafendorf during the 1960s and early 1970s offered a fascinating, if rather melancholy view of the ÖBB's varied narrow gauge steam locomotive classes. Happily, many of them would enjoy a fresh lease of life – in a few rare instances through a return to the active ranks of the ÖBB fleet, but more often in preservation.

In September 1963, No 499.01 (Krauss, Linz 1262/1924), an especially interesting locomotive which spent many years at Obergrafendorf, is still in a relatively good condition. Although it arrived as early as 1963, like many of the locomotives at Obergrafendorf No 499.01 would not officially be withdrawn until March 1973. It later became part of the collection at the preserved section of the Gurktalbahn. *Author's Collection*

Although a successful design, No 398.01 (Krauss, Linz 5330/1905) remained a one-off. It was last allocated to Gmünd on the Waldviertelbahn. Although it came to Obergrafendorf in the 1960s, No 398.01 was one of the many narrow gauge steam locomotives which were officially withdrawn on 15 March 1973, after which it was acquired by railway preservation society *Club 760*. As part of an exchange of locomotives it passed to the Steiermärkische Landesbahnen, which restored it to use as No Bh 1 operating tourist services on the Murtalbahn. *Author's Collection*

Also present in September 1963 was No 898.01 (Henschel 25702/1941), a 0-6-0T, built as a demonstration locomotive for the German *Heeresfeldbahn*. First operated as HF 20751 in the war zones of Yugoslavia, in 1944 it was transferred to St Pölten Alpenbahnhof, where it was put to work from 1945 on shunting duties. In 1953 it became No 898.01 under the new ÖBB numbering scheme. Its working days at an end, it was moved to Obergrafendorf in December 1965, but in 1971 it was sold for preservation on static display. *Author's Collection*

Above: Another locomotive to be found at Obergrafendorf in September 1963 was ÖBB No 298.103 (Krauss, Linz 1995/1889), which was built as No 3 *Grünburg* of the Steyrtalbahn, where it spent its entire working life. No 298.103 was the first of the original Steyrtalbahn locomotives to find its way to the narrow gauge dump at Obergrafendorf, where it arrived in May 1963. Official withdrawal followed soon afterwards on 2 August 1963. *Author's Collection*

Opposite above: Seen in 1969, No 998.01 (Krauss, München 7651/1920), the former No HF 200, was moved to Obergrafendorf in 1966. During World War 2 it had made its way to the territory of today's Austria via the German *Heeresfeldbahn*, numbered 11200, and after 1945 it operated on the Pinzgauer Lokalbahn between Zell am See and Krimml, where its last duties, as a reserve locomotive, ended in October 1964. After slumbering at Obergrafendorf for many years, it was acquired for preservation. *Author's Collection*

Opposite below: Class 498 No 498.07 (Floridsdorf 3037/1931), originally delivered as BBÖ No Uh 101, operated on the Steyrtalbahn from July 1966. After being taken out of service at Garsten in 1967, No 498.07 was moved to Obergrafendorf, where it is seen in 1969. Officially withdrawn on 15 March 1973, it was later put on static display. *Author's Collection*

12. The Murtalbahn (StmLB)

Opened in 1894, the Murtalbahn, running 76.2km from Unzmarkt, on the main line between Leoben and Klagenfurt, to Mauterndorf, was Austria's second-longest narrow gauge railway. The operational centre and workshops were located at Murau, 26.9km from Unzmarkt. In July 1942, the Murtalbahn was taken over by the local government of Steiermark, after which it was operated by the Steiermärkische Landesbahnen. The poor financial performance of the last 11km between Tamsweg and Mauterndorf led to passenger services on this section ending in 1973.

From the opening of the line until the start of diesel services some 70 years later, members of the famous 'U' class were the foundation of services on the Murtalbahn. The class letter U – for Unzmarkt – derives from the fact that it was on the Murtalbahn that the class was first introduced in 1894. Subsequently the 'U' class was used in large numbers on narrow gauge railways in many parts of the Austro-Hungarian empire. Although the 'U' class was for many years symbolic of the Murtalbahn, other locomotives also featured. Especially worthy of mention are the StmLB's two powerful 0-10-0Ts, Nos Kh 101 and Kh 111.

Diesel traction was introduced from 1964, but the steam era had not yet ended. Four years later the Murtalbahn began a programme of steam-hauled excursion trains, which soon achieved considerable popularity, and starting in 1969 driver experience courses using small 0-4-0T No 2 *Stainz* were another successful development.

On 7 May 1959 No U40 (Wiener Neustadt 4870/1908) stands at Murau with train No UM 52, the 7.09am departure for Unzmarkt. The train departed Mauterndorf at 4.45am, and is due to reach Unzmarkt at 8.15am – a journey time of some 3½ hours for a distance of 76km. *Charles Firminger/Online Transport Archive*

No U40 stands at Niederwölz with its mixed train. No U40 and seven classmates were originally built for the Triest – Parenzo railway. Together with Nos U37 and U38, however, it moved in 1911 to the newly built Feistritztalbahn from Weiz to Birkfeld, and was later transferred to the Steiermärkische Landesbahnen. *Charles Firminger/Online Transport Archive*

The train has arrived at Unzmarkt; No U40 is attended to by its crew, and has its supplies of coal and water replenished. *Charles Firminger/Online Transport Archive*

Opposite above: No U11 (Krauss, Linz 3065/1894) stands on a train at Unzmarkt in July 1961. The main line can be seen on the left. No U11 was delivered with four sister locomotives for the opening of the Murtalbahn in 1894, and was originally named *Mauterndorf*. *Phil Tatt/Online Transport Archive*

Opposite below: No U11 is replaced at Murau by classmate U40. Whilst No U40 awaits the order to depart, No U11 runs light engine to the shed. *Phil Tatt/Online Transport Archive*

Right: No Kh 111 (Krauss, Linz 1519/1930), originally built for the Feistritztalbahn, was later transferred to the Murtalbahn. An unusual feature was its Caprotti valve gear. In September 1963 it is seen running round its train at Mauterndorf. *Author's Collection*

Above: 0-4-0T No 2 *Stainz* was one of the smallest steam locomotives to be operated on Austria's public narrow gauge railways. Two examples each were built in 1892 for both the Preding-Wieselsdorf – Stainz local railway and the Pöltschach – Gonobitz local railway, located in what was then Untersteiermark (Lower Styria), part of the present day Slovenia. After being taken out of service in the 1950s, *Stainz* was initially kept in reserve.

In 1967 it received an overhaul in the StmLB workshops at Weiz, during which a number of modifications were carried out. These included conversion to superheating, and fitting a second set of the main controls on the fireman's side of the footplate, enabling driver experience courses to be introduced on the Murtalbahn from 1969 using *Stainz*. *Author's Collection*

13. The Feistritztalbahn (StmLB)

The Feistritztalbahn, which opened in December 1911, ran 23.9km from Weiz, where it connected with the standard gauge line from Gleisdorf, to Birkfeld. An 18.3km extension to the lignite mine at Ratten opened in 1922 – initially as a simple industrial siding. The mine closed in 1960, and a decline in the level of passenger traffic led in February 1971 to the closure of the Birkfeld to Ratten section, followed in June 1973 by the end of passenger services between Weiz and Birkfeld, although significant goods traffic continued. The line featured a number of impressive viaducts, amongst which the largest was the 276m long Grub viaduct.

For many years the line was operated largely by the near-universal 'U' class. Especially worthy of mention is No U38, the only member of the class to carry a Giesl ejector, which was unfortunately scrapped after being involved in a serious derailment when it ran into a landslide in August 1962, ending up in the river Feistritz. After the impressive 0-10-0T No Kh 101 was built for the Murtalbahn in 1926, the closely related No Kh 111 was delivered to the Feistritztalbahn in 1930, differing from its predecessor primarily through the use of Caprotti valve gear. In 1943 No Kh 111 was transferred from Weiz to Murau.

In 1955 the Steiermärkische Landesbahnen acquired No 19 of the Salzmammergut-Lokalbahn, a former *Heeresfeldbahn* 'KDL 11' type 0-8-0TT, which it rebuilt with full-length side tanks and without a tender, becoming StmLB No 699.01. Relatively little used, it was sold in 1969. Following the closure of the Salzkammergut-Lokalbahn in 1957, the StmLB acquired three of its distinctive 0-6-2Ts, Nos 7, 11 and 12, which the StmLB fitted with extended side tanks. Nos 7 and 12 operated on the Feistritztalbahn as Nos S7 and S12. In 1966 No S7 was fitted with a 'U' class boiler, complete with a typical 'U' class spark arresting chimney, leaving it unrecognisable as a former SKGLB locomotive. The arrival of powerful diesels in 1967 led to the end of steam traction, except on tourist trains.

On 3 September 1963, the former No 12 of the Salzkammergut-Lokalbahn, No S12 of the Steiermärkische Landesbahnen, awaits departure from Weiz, where the narrow gauge platform was situated on the station forecourt of the standard gauge StmLB line from Gleisdorf. When No S12 first arrived in the Feistritz valley it retained its traditional appearance, but by now it has gained extended side tanks, like sister locomotives Nos S7 and S11. No S12 operated on the Feistritztalbahn between 1958 and 1965. *Author's Collection*

Above: No 699.01 (Franco Belge 2855/1944) stands outside the locomotive shed at Ratten on the gloomy 20 May 1964. In 1955 the Steiermärkische Landesbahnen acquired the former *Heeresfeldbahn* HF 2855, No 19 of the Salzkammergut-Lokalbahn, fitted it with a new copper firebox and rebuilt it as a tank locomotive putting it into service as StmLB No 699.01. *Charles Firminger/Online Transport Archive*

Below: No 699.01 waits at Anger with its train from Ratten to Weiz. No 699.01 was not especially popular on the Feistritztalbahn, and was not greatly used. After standing out of use at Weiz for some time, in 1969 it was sold to the Welshpool & Llanfair Light Railway. No 699.01 should not be confused with the very similar ÖBB Class 699, and never operated on the ÖBB. *Charles Firminger/Online Transport Archive*

Left: No U7 (Krauss, Linz 4138/1899) is seen in the 1960s at the head of a typical Feistritztalbahn passenger train of the period. *Author's Collection*

Below: No U7 has arrived at the attractively located roadside halt at Rosegg, 17.4km from Weiz. *Author's Collection*

Heading down the valley towards Weiz, a train double-headed by Nos U8 (Krauss, Linz 3062/1894) and S12 (Krauss, Linz 5513/1906), stands in the evening sun at Oberfeistritz in the early 1960s. *Author's Collection*

14. The Lokalbahn Kapfenberg – Au-Seewiesen, Thörlerbahn (StmLB)

The Lokalbahn Kapfenberg – Au-Seewiesen, also known as the Thörlerbahn, was a 760mm gauge railway, opened in 1893, which ran 22.7km from Kapfenberg, on the main line between Leoben and Mürzzuschlag, to Au-Seewiesen. Its principal traffic came from the iron and forestry industries, and passenger traffic ended as early as March 1959. As a result of a decline in the timber traffic from Au-Seewiesen, the last 3km from Seebach-Turnau to Au-Seewiesen were closed in 1964, and the tracks were removed, but significant freight traffic continued on the remaining section.

Three small 0-6-0T locomotives, Nos 5-7, were supplied for the opening of the line in 1893, which were almost identical to the Pinzgauer Lokalbahn 'Z' class. The last example, No 6, remained in traffic at Kapfenberg into the 1960s. In 1896 support arrived in the form of 'U' class No 12 *Graz*, which operated on the Thörlerbahn until withdrawal in 1969. Like Nos 5-7, its number had no class prefix letter. No U44 (Krauss, Linz 1257/1922), the last built member of the famous 'U' class, worked at Kapfenberg from 1943 until 1964, as did classmate No U7 (Krauss, Linz 4138/1899) from 1945 until 1947.

Various interesting locomotives found their way to Kapfenberg over the years. No 502 was an unusual superheated 0-10-0T, built by Maffei in 1920, which was acquired by the StmLB in 1928, and operated until 1939 on the Feistritztalbahn. In use at Kapfenberg for many years, it was finally scrapped in 1965. No 11805, one of three former *Heeresfeldbahn* Class HF 110C locomotives, acquired by the StmLB in 1949, operated at Kapfenberg until 1965. Following the StmLB's acquisition of three of the classic Salzkammergut-Lokalbahn 0-6-2Ts subsequent to the closure of the SKGLB in 1957, No 11 found a new home on the Thörlerbahn as No S11 from 1958 to 1967.

Although the first diesel had arrived at Kapfenberg in 1958, powerful 0-10-0T No Kh 101, built for the Murtalbahn in 1926, was nonetheless transferred to the Thörlerbahn in 1965. When one of the large StmLB diesels entered service in 1968, the days of steam traction appeared numbered, but No Kh 101 nonetheless remained in use until the 1970s.

No Kh 101 (Krauss, Linz 1419/1926) is seen shunting at Kapfenberg Landesbahn station in 1965. A superheated, 10-coupled locomotive, its design was based on BBÖ No Kh 1, which was built in 1924 for the Lokalbahn Kühnsdorf-Eisenkappel. No Kh 101 was built in 1926 for the Murtalbahn, and transferred to Kapfenberg in 1965. *Author's Collection*

Above: StmLB No 6 (Krauss, Linz 2885/1893), the last survivor of the three 0-6-0Ts that were built in 1893 for the opening of the Kapfenberg to Au-Seewiesen line, seen at Kapfenberg in 1965.
Author's Collection

Below: On 14 October 1972, No Kh 101 stands with a goods train at Seebach-Turnau, terminus of the Thörlerbahn since 1964.
Author's Collection

15. The Zillertalbahn

The 760mm gauge Zillertalbahn was built to connect the communities of the Ziller valley with the Innsbruck-Wörgl main line at Jenbach. It was opened in stages from the end of 1900, with the last section, from Zell am Ziller to Mayrhofen (32.9km from Jenbach), opening in July 1902. It played an important role in transporting wood and magnesite, and gained a new prominence between 1967 and 1971 in delivering materials and equipment for the construction of a hydro-electric power station at Mayrhofen. A short connecting line was built for this purpose, diverging from the existing line just before Mayrhofen station, leading to a specially created freight yard, and continuing to the power station. A large number of freights ran each day, in particular as many as five cement trains.

At the time of opening, the locomotive fleet consisted of two members of the 'U' class – No 1 *Raimund* and No 2 *Zillerthal*. Two years later they were reinforced with the arrival of No 3 *Tirol*, a larger and more powerful compound locomotive belonging to Class Uv. An unusual further addition was No 4 *Gerlos*, a small 2-4-0T compound, built by Krauss, Linz in 1905. Next, in 1930, came No 5, a 'Uh' class superheated 0-6-2T, which was a development of the 'U' class. No 5 was the last steam locomotive to be built by Krauss at Linz before the Linz works closed its doors.

In 1958 the first No 4 was replaced by a very different locomotive – a former *Heeresfeldbahn* 0-10-0TT, built by Borsig in 1939 as No HF 191, which had been rendered redundant by the closure of the famous Salzkammergut-Lokalbahn in 1957. Formerly SKGLB No 22, on arrival at the Zillertalbahn it became the line's second No 4. The imposing and powerful Borsig locomotive would remain on the Zillertalbahn until 1974.

Below: Zillertalbahn No 3 (Krauss, Linz 4790/1902) stands in the magnificent setting at Schlitters with a train to Mayrhofen, including traditional Zillertalbahn four-wheel coaches, on 17 August 1956. *John McCann/Online Transport Archive*

Opposite: A head-on view of No 3 illustrates the difference in size between the high pressure cylinder (on the left in the picture) and the low pressure cylinder (on the right). *John McCann/Online Transport Archive*

Right: On 17 August 1956, No 3 is seen at Zell am Ziller shunting two open goods wagons loaded with timber. *John McCann/Online Transport Archive*

Below: The well occupied train awaits the return of No 3 from its shunting activities before continuing its journey towards Jenbach. *John McCann/Online Transport Archive*

Above: No 2 (Krauss, Linz 4506/1900) stands at Jenbach depot in the 1950s, ready for its next turn of duty.
Author's Collection

Right: All looks well, but time is running out for unusual 2-4-0T compound No 4 (Krauss, Linz 5355/1905), seen on shunting duties at Jenbach. When the former SKGLB No 22 was acquired by the Zillertalbahn and put to work as the new No 4, the original No 4 went the opposite way, being taken to the former SKGLB workshops at Salzburg Itzling for scrapping.
Author's Collection

Opposite above: Superheated 0-6-2T No 5 (Krauss, Linz 1521/1930), hurries towards Jenbach with a passenger train. The interesting train formation includes two of the four former Lokalbahn Payerbach – Hirschwang coaches built by the Grazer Waggonfabrik, which were acquired by the Zillertalbahn after the end of passenger services on the LBPH in 1963, as well as a traditional eight-window Zillertalbahn coach and two modern bogie coaches. *Author's Collection*

Opposite below: The second No 4 (Borsig 14806/1939) is seen shunting at Mayrhofen. Previously SKGLB No 22, it came to the Zillertalbahn in 1958, with the first No 4 departing in part exchange. The 0-10-0TT remained on the Zillertalbahn until 1974. *Author's Collection*

Above: A train for Jenbach departs from the station at Ramsau im Zillertal on a bright winter's day in February 1963. *Marc Dahlström*

16. The Achenseebahn

The Achenseebahn, a metre gauge rack railway, opened in June 1889. The 6.36km-long line led from Jenbach (elevation 530m) on the Wörgl-Innsbruck main line, via the mid-way point and summit at Eben (3.6km, elevation 970m) to Seespitz am Achensee (elevation 931m). In 1929 the line was extended by 400m, reaching its final length of 6.76km.

The main incline, with a maximum gradient of 16% (1 in 6.2), which was equipped with the Riggenbach rack system, was located between Jenbach and Eben, beginning immediately after departing the station at Jenbach. From the summit at Eben the line descended gently to Maurach, continuing from there to the terminus at Seespitz am Achensee, where the trains connected with the pleasure craft on the lake.

On the rack section between Jenbach and Eben the train was propelled by the locomotive. At Eben the locomotive ran round its train before hauling it for the rest of the journey. In the opposite direction the train was hauled for the entire journey, so that on the rack section the locomotive was always at the downhill end of the train.

From the opening of the line the motive power fleet consisted of the four identical locomotives, Nos 1–4, originally named *Theodor*, *Hermann*, *Georg* and *Carl*, which were supplied by Lokomotivfabrik Floridsdorf. No 4 was taken out of service in 1930, and following World War 2 it was used as a source of spare parts for Nos 1–3.

Achenseebahn No 1 pauses at Eben with a train consisting of a single coach, before continuing its journey on the level section. *John McCann/Online Transport Archive*

Above: No 1 (Floridsdorf 701/1889) stands beside the locomotive shed at Jenbach on 12 September 1958. *John McCann/Online Transport Archive*

Right: Having propelled its train up the 16% (1 in 6.2) incline from Jenbach, No 1 runs round at Eben on 12 September 1958. *John McCann/Online Transport Archive*

Above: After 4.8km, No 1 has arrived with its RCTS special train at Maurach. *John McCann/Online Transport Archive*

Opposite above: In the picturesque setting of the Achensee, No 2 (Floridsdorf 702/1889) waits for the return to Jenbach on the evening of 12 September 1958. *John McCann/Online Transport Archive*

Opposite below: Leaving Jenbach with an engineering train in the autumn of 1964, No 1 has just joined the rack section. *Author's Collection*

Steam in Industry

Although often overshadowed by railways operating public services, the industrial railways of Austria had a great deal to offer the enthusiast. Rail operations were a feature of various industrial locations, including sugar factories, paper mills and chemical works, breweries and gasworks, but particularly sites operated by the most significant industries – iron & steel, coal and timber. On forestry railways, where different types of internal combustion locomotive were often employed, steam power tended to have less significance in later years, but there were some interesting exceptions, such as the 22km long 600mm gauge Steinhaus – Rettenegg forestry railway, which featured two charming 0-6-0Ts from Krauss, Linz (1918) and Decauville (1926) until its closure in 1958.

The iron ore mining operations at the famous 'Iron Mountain' in Steiermark featured a variety of locomotives on different gauges – primarily 830mm and 900mm (previously 920mm). Especially worthy of mention is the 830mm gauge Radmer forest railway, which carried timber (until 1956), and in later years exclusively iron ore, through a remote and wild area to the south of Hieflau. Between 1962 and 1967, three former ÖBB Class 498 locomotives were used on the Radmer

system, re-gauged from 760mm to 830mm, as Nos 14/200, 15/200 and 16/200, but these did not meet with great success.

Steam power ruled supreme on the rail systems of the iron & steel industry into the 1970s. The two largest operations served the enormous steelworks at Linz and Donawitz, both of which featured a wide range of locomotives, consisting not just of industrial types, but also including a number of examples acquired second-hand from the public railways. As was the case at some of the smaller iron & steel sites, steam traction continued at Linz and Donawitz into the 1970s, but then went into severe decline, principally because of its replacement with diesel locomotives, but also in consequence of rationalisation and closures in the steel industry.

Smartly turned-out locomotive No 3 of the Wolfsegg-Traunthaler Kohlenwerks AG (Floridsdorf 9493/1944) is seen at Ampflwang on 14 May 1972. *Author's Collection*

1. VÖEST Linz

During World War 2, a large steelworks with several blast furnaces was built at Linz to create additional steel production capacity, and together with increased iron ore output from the 'Iron Mountain' to contribute to the war effort. In July 1946, the steelworks at Linz was nationalised and renamed as VÖEST (Vereinigte Österreichische Eisen- und Stahlwerke). In the post-war years, the facilities were rebuilt and expanded, with the VÖEST business being the recipient of the largest single capital injection to be made in Austria under the Marshall Plan, and during the following years, it enjoyed a period of continuous growth. From 1952, the introduction of the new Linz-Donawitz (LD) process transformed steel production, thanks to a shortened manufacturing time and reduced capital cost per tonne of steel, largely supplanting the previous processes worldwide, with the world's first steelworks using the LD process being built at Linz.

In the 1970s, the VÖEST and the Österreichisch-Alpine Montangesellschaft (operator of the huge steelworks at Leoben-Donawitz) companies, as well as Schoeller-Bleckmann Stahlwerke AG,

Gebrüder Böhler & Co AG, and Steirische Gußstahlwerke AG, were merged to form a national Austrian steel concern, with the name Voest-Alpine AG.

The VÖEST site at Linz featured an extensive railway system, which operated a large and interesting fleet of steam locomotives.

During the 1950s and 1960s the ÖBB operated a number of interesting locomotives of German origin. Amongst these were four powerful superheated 0-8-0Ts, originally built for the Lübeck-Büchener Eisenbahn, where they were numbered 123-126. In ÖBB ownership they became Nos 692.431-434. All four locomotives were sold in December 1963 to the VÖEST steelworks at Linz, where they retained their ÖBB identities. No 692.434 (Linke-Hofmann 2675/1925), seen at Linz in 1969, was withdrawn in November 1973. *Author's Collection*

2. ÖAMG Donawitz

The enormous steelworks at Donawitz lies on the north-west side of Leoben in the Obersteiermark region, and owes its existence to the massive iron ore reserves of the nearby *Erzberg* or 'Iron Mountain'. The coming of the industrial revolution, and the introduction of steam power, led to a considerable increase in output, which rapidly grew further with connection to the railway network in 1868. The amalgamation of various steelworks in 1881 gave rise to the Österreichisch-Alpine Montangesellschaft (ÖAMG), with its centre at Donawitz. In the first years of the 20th century the expansion of the operations at Donawitz continued, and as a result of demand generated by the war effort in World War 1, production of pig iron reached a peak of more than 410,000 tonnes in 1916. The fall of the Habsburg monarchy at the end of the war resulted in a drastic reduction in potential sales markets, which was exacerbated by the worldwide economic crisis of the 1930s. However, World War 2 led once again to greatly increased production volumes, and in 1941 output was expanded to approximately 500,000 tonnes to meet the demands of the arms industry. Unlike the VÖEST steelworks at Linz, Donawitz was spared extensive damage as a consequence of air raids during World War 2.

Under the Austrian Iron & Steel Plan of 1948, the other major steelworks at Linz would in future produce flat products (sheet metal), whilst Donawitz would specialise in the production of steel profile, girders, rails and wire. In 1973 the ÖAMG business was merged with the Vereinigte Österreichische Eisen- und Stahlwerke (VÖEST) and other iron & steel producers, creating the national steel manufacturer Voest-Alpine AG.

Until the 1970s the steelworks at Donawitz featured a varied assortment of steam locomotives – both on the narrow gauge lines, with the unusual gauge of 790mm, and the standard gauge; the latter including second-hand locomotives sourced from both the ÖBB and the Graz-Köflacher Bahn. The 790mm system ceased operations in 1974, and steam operations on the standard gauge ended in April 1975, with the arrival at Donawitz of 12 newly-built diesels.

Diminutive 790mm gauge No 40.2 (Krauss, Linz 5938/1908) is seen at Donawitz on 7 September 1963. The run-down of the narrow gauge system at Donawitz in the 1970s brought the withdrawal of No 40.2 in 1970. *Author's Collection*

No 100.13 (Floridsdorf 17609/1947) was one of a series of three 790mm gauge locomotives delivered to Donawitz by Floridsdorf in 1947. It is seen in 1972 on one of the many sharp curves to be found about the site. The numbering scheme for steam locomotives at Donawitz featured a prefix denoting the locomotive's power in horsepower, followed by the individual running number.
Author's Collection

Veteran 2-6-2T Nr 600.2 (Wiener Neustadt 4027/1897), was one of two members of the class which came to Donawitz from the Graz-Köflacher Bahn. Built in 1897 as kkStB No 3033, it was acquired by the GKB in October 1934 as No 30.33. On 29 March 1961 it changed owner again when it moved to the ÖAMG system at Donawitz, where it is seen in 1969.
Author's Collection

3. Wolfsegg-Traunthaler Kohlenwerks AG (Ampflwanger Bahn)

The brown coal (lignite) mining industry in the Hausruck region of Oberösterreich, which began at the end of the 18th century, led in 1856 to the founding of a firm which would later become the Wolfsegg-Traunthaler Kohlenwerks Aktiengesellschaft (WTK). In 1920 an 11km long 600mm gauge industrial railway was constructed from Ampflwang to Timelkam on the main line between Salzburg and Linz. In the 1920s a power station was built at Timelkam, which was fed with brown coal from Ampflwang, and the line was converted to standard gauge in 1924 in order to increase its capacity. A restricted passenger service was introduced on the WTK during World War 2, with the purpose of transporting employees of the railway, mines and power station, and their relatives, as well as school children, and for many years most trains between Timelkam and Ampflwang ran as mixed services, with a passenger carriage coupled next to the locomotive.

Three 0-8-0Ts were obtained for the opening of the standard gauge line in 1925. Nos 1 and 2, built by Krauss, Linz, corresponded to the numerous kkStB Class 178 (later ÖBB Class 92). The third was an elegant product of Henschel at Kassel. During World War 2, WTK No 1 was transferred to the Oberösterreichische Kraftwerke AG,

operator of the power station at Timelkam, and was replaced by a further 0-8-0T – this time a superheated locomotive from Floridsdorf, built to the same design as BBÖ Class 478 (later ÖBB Class 392). It became WTK No 3, and in 1959 was fitted with a Giesl ejector. In 1966 a genuine Class 392 locomotive was purchased from the ÖBB; this being ÖBB No 392.2539 of 1927, which became WTK No 4. Until 1977 locomotives belonging to the power station company were responsible for shunting the power station sidings at Timelkam, where they could often be seen side-by-side with WTK locomotives. Until the first diesel arrived at the WTK in 1973, services were entirely steam operated, but in 1977 a second diesel was delivered, which spelled the end of steam traction.

The well-proportioned Hanomag (9976/1923) is seen stabled at Ampflwang on 24 May 1972. *Author's Collection*

Above: No 2 (Krauss, Linz 1400/1925), standing out of use at Ampflwang in 1969, had been fitted with a Giesl ejector in 1959, and was officially withdrawn in 1971. *Author's Collection*

Right: WTK No 3 (Floridsdorf 9493/1944), seen with a special train for British railway enthusiasts, was scrapped in 1973 without reaching its 30th birthday. *Author's Collection*

4. Schoeller-Bleckmann Stahlwerke AG (Mürzzuschlag – Hönigsberg)

Steel company Schoeller-Bleckmann Stahlwerke AG at Mürzzuschlag in Steiermark had both standard and 760mm gauge operations; the standard gauge lines connecting with the adjacent ÖBB line. Both standard and narrow gauge lines ran from the steelworks at Mürzzuschlag to another SBS site in the nearby suburb of Hönigsberg. From 1931 until 1971 the narrow gauge line operated a restricted passenger service, not for public use, which was used to transport SBS employees. With the closure of the narrow gauge system, this service was transferred to the standard gauge system from 1972.

On the standard gauge there were two 0-6-0Ts, built by Floridsdorf, which differed in age by more than 30 years. These were *Phönix* (2678/1920) and a modern Giesl-fitted locomotive (17689/1952), which was appropriately known as *Die Neue* ('the new one'). Correspondingly, *Phönix* was often known by staff as *Die Alte*

('the old one'). The narrow gauge system was operated by several small 0-4-0Ts. The last of these, in the final years until the end of narrow gauge operations, were a pair of locomotives named *Wolf* and *Hans*, which operated together with several small diesels.

SBS locomotives large and small. 760mm gauge 0-4-0WT *Hans* (Zobel 637/1913) stands outside the shared standard and narrow gauge locomotive shed at Mürzzuschlag. Beside *Hans* is the modern standard gauge 0-6-0T known as *Die Neue* (Floridsdorf 17689/1952). The diminutive size of the SBS narrow gauge locomotives and stock is apparent. The reason why such a small locomotive was fitted with a Giesl ejector lies in the fact that Schoeller-Bleckmann manufactured and held the licence for the Giesl ejector. *Author's Collection*

Above: The second 760mm gauge steam locomotive in use at Schoeller-Bleckmann in the 1960s was another small 0-4-0WT, named *Wolf* (Krauss, Linz 4928/1902), seen waiting for passengers with one of the internal services operated for use by SBS employees. *Author's Collection*

Below: Wolf, seen with a passenger train between Mürzzuschlag and Hönigsberg on an early summer's day, remained in use until 1971 as the last steam locomotive to operate on the Schoeller-Bleckmann 760mm gauge system. *Author's Collection*

5. Steirische Gußstahlwerke AG – Judenburg

Until the 1970s, the Steirische Gußstahlwerke (Styrian Cast Steel Works) company operated two standard gauge tank locomotives and a small but interesting fleet of second-hand 760mm gauge locomotives at its works at Judenburg in Steiermark, situated just to the west of Zeltweg and Knittelfeld in the Mur valley.

In 1975, Steirische Gußstahlwerke AG, Schoeller-Bleckmann Stahlwerke AG and Gebrüder Böhler & Co AG (Böhler Werke), were amalgamated to become the Vereinigte Edelstahlwerke AG (VEW), a wholly owned subsidiary of Voest-Alpine AG.

On an extremely wet spring day in 1972, purposeful looking 0-4-0T No 170.4 *Lisl* (Krauss Maffei 17834/1952) stands in steam at Judenburg. *Author's Collection*

Above: Lisl was transferred to Judenburg in 1960 from the Österreichisch-Alpine Montangesellschaft (ÖAMG) at Donawitz. Originally built for the 790mm gauge system at Donawitz, *Lisl* had to be re-gauged to 760mm for use at Judenburg. *Author's Collection*

Right: On the same day, charming 0-4-0T *Hanni* (Krauss, Linz 1342/1926) is also seen in operation on the 760mm gauge system at Judenburg. Originally built as a 0-6-0T, *Hanni* came to Judenburg in 1965 from the Steyrermühl paper mill. *Author's Collection*

Bubliography/Further Reading

Books

100 Jahre Feistritztalbahn	Karl Schellauf, Dietmar Zehetner
125 Jahre Steyrtalbahn	Raimund Ločičnik
Auf Schmalspurgleisen durch das Zillertal	Dr Stefan Lueginger
Bahn im Bild – various volumes	Verlag Pospischil
Dampfbetrieb in Österreich – volumes 1 & 2	Eduard Saßmann
Dampfgetriebene Triebfahrzeuge – volumes 1-5	Johann Blieberger, Josef Pospichal
Dampflokomotiven auf der Steyrtalbahn	Wilhelm Tausche
Der Giesl-Ejektor	Josef Otto Slezak
Der Schneeberg und seine Bahn	Dr Alfred Niel
Die Feistritztalbahn Weiz – Birkfeld – Ratten	Alfred Luft
Die Feistritztalbahn: Schmalspurreise durch die Oststeiermark	Dr Alfred Niel
Die Goldene Zeit der ÖBB	Wolfgang Kaiser
Die Gurktalbahn	Dieter Stanfel
Die Pinzgauer Lokalbahn	Herbert Fritz
Die Waldviertler Schmalspurbahn	Werner Schiendl
Eisenbahn Bilderalbum – various volumes	Alfred Horn
Eisenbahnatlas Österreich	Schweers & Wahl
Eisenbahnen am Steirischen Erzberg	Manfred Hohn
Fahrzeugportrait Reihe U	Roland Beier
KDL 11 Kriegsdampflokomotive 11	Herbert Fritz
Mit Sack und Pack nach Pfaffenschlag	Werner Schiendl
Schafbergbahn und Wolfgangseeschiffe	Gunter Mackinger
Schmalspurig durch Österreich	Dr Walter Krobot, Josef Otto Slezak, Hans Sternhart
Steyrtalbahn	Christian Hager, Peter Wegenstein
Unvergessene Thörlerbahn	Dietmar Zehetner
Volldampf auf der Erzbergbahn	Carl Asmus, Johann Stockklausner, Albert Ditterich
Von Salzburg nach Bad Ischl	Josef Otto Slezak
Waldbahnen in Österreich	Manfred Hohn
Wege aus Eisen – various volumes	Peter Wegenstein
Ybbstalbahn	Dieter Stanfel

Magazine Specials

Eisenbahn Journal ÖBB in den 70ern	Matthias Wiener
Eisenbahn Journal Eisenbahn in Österreich ÖBB 1945-1970	Andres Knipping

Web-sites

www.pospichal.net
www.gkb.at
www.heeresfeldbahn.de

No 93.1414 departs from Schwarzenau on 18 February 1975. *Author's Collection*